PRAISE FOR *PLANS FOR YOUR GOOD*

"Prime Minister Scott Morrison proved his strength in leadership, standing up for freedom and staring down the aggressive coercion of the People's Republic of China in the Indo-Pacific. He has written a book about the essence of humanity and God's will. He has also told an epic tale about how one man can lead a family and a nation with dignity, decency, and faith. It's also fun, so read, learn, and enjoy."

> SECRETARY MIKE POMPEO, 70th US Secretary of State;
> former Director of the Central Intelligence Agency

"*Plans for Your Good* unveils the often unseen yet essential element of a world leader's decision-making—faith. From building a family to leading a country to conquering fear in the face of rising adversaries and spearheading the transformative AUKUS security partnership, Prime Minister Morrison proves the power of prayer and challenges us to nurture our relationship with the Lord. This is a must-read for leaders who want to build their career on a foundation of faith."

> CONGRESSMAN MIKE GALLAGHER, Chair of the House
> Committee on the Communist Party of China

"Laden with truth and rich with real world experience, Scott takes us on a journey through his own story to remind us that real faith is about a life of obedience. He calls us all to take action in the circumstances in which we find ourselves and to have the courage to live the life God has for you. Take this book seriously and it will equip you for your adventure of a lifetime."

> BARONESS PHILIPPA STROUD, UK House of Lords; Chief
> Executive, Alliance for Responsible Citizenship

"As Prime Minister of Australia from 2018 to 2022, Scott Morrison led his country through the COVID-19 pandemic and a time of rapidly growing international tension. In his readable and engaging memoir, *Plans for Your Good*, he reveals the Christian faith that shaped his remarkable journey from family man to Prime Minister and guided him through turbulent times. The world needs more political leaders who walk humbly with their God; let us hope that Scott's story will inspire others to follow in his footsteps."

WALTER RUSSELL MEAD, author of *Special Providence: American Foreign Policy and How It Changed the World*; Distinguished Fellow at Hudson Institute; *Wall Street Journal* columnist and professor of foreign affairs and humanities, Bard College, New York

"*Plans for Your Good* really spoke to me about God's purposes for our lives. Prime Minister Morrison's moral conviction led him to oppose even those who afforded and sustained him in power. Scott Morrison's moral courage was never in doubt."

KELLY CRAFT, US Ambassador to the United Nations (2019–2021) and Canada (2017–2019)

"Here is a unique insight into a Prime Minister's mind, a mind so it turns out which is full of God, Scripture and the Spirit. This companionable book offers unique insights into the interaction of public policy and personal spirituality. It is filled with gems of wisdom."

GREG SHERIDAN, foreign editor for *The Australian*; author of *Christians: The Urgent Case for Jesus in Our World*

"Scott Morrison has written a book that surprises as it unpacks both the great internal and external challenges of our civilizational moment in ways that demand the attention of both those who are engaged and those many who are unwisely disengaged in these dangerous times.

As a former national leader, his insights into the collapse of belief in our own story, and the way this interplays with what he has referred to as the 'arc of autocracy' that loathes the West, are of great importance. His courage and vision in the development of AUKUS reflects his determination to do all he could to 'walk' his 'talk'."

HON. JOHN ANDERSON AC FTSE, Deputy Prime Minister of Australia (1999–2005)

Plans
for
Your Good

Plans *for* *Your* Good

A Prime Minister's
Testimony of God's
Faithfulness

SCOTT MORRISON
30th Prime Minister of Australia

W PUBLISHING GROUP

AN IMPRINT OF THOMAS NELSON

Published in Nashville, Tennessee, by W Publishing, an imprint of Thomas Nelson.

Thomas Nelson titles may be purchased in bulk for educational, business, fundraising, or sales promotional use. For information, please email SpecialMarkets@ ThomasNelson.com.

ISBN 978-1-4003-4031-6 (audiobook)
ISBN 978-1-4003-4030-9 (eBook)
ISBN 978-1-4003-4028-6 (HC)

Library of Congress Control Number: 2023941254

Printed in the United States of America
24 25 26 27 28 LBC 5 4 3 2 1

To Jen, with love and thanksgiving

CONTENTS

FOREWORD

Australia and the United States have a long history of strategic partnership (or as the Aussies call it, "mateship.") For more than a century, friendship between our two countries has made the world a safer and more prosperous place.

In 1918, Australians and Americans first fought side by side to liberate the French town of Le Hamel from Nazi occupation during the First World War. While the Battle of Midway is well remembered as the turning point for the Pacific theater in the Second World War, there would have been no Midway had not our two countries worked together to successfully turn back the Japanese advance into New Guinea during the Battle of the Coral Sea a month earlier. In 1951, we signed a security treaty; half a century later, when terrorists killed twenty-two Australians and thousands of Americans, Australia honored that treaty as one of the first countries to come to our aid.

Given the strength and character of our national partnership, it's only fitting that, when Prime Minister Scott Morrison and I first met in 2018 during my service as Vice President of the United States, we also became prayer partners. There is an old saying that "when Christians clasp their hands in prayer, it is the beginning of an uprising against the disorder of the world." Well, there was plenty of worldly disorder to talk about at that first meeting: North Korea going nuclear, China tightening its grip on the South China Sea, and Venezuela's rigged elections to reelect a thug dictator.

So, when we had concluded our official bilateral talks, we turned to the most important work we could do on behalf of our countries: prayer. Together, we prayed over everything we had just discussed. As Scott makes clear in this book, and as the Christian faith has long proclaimed, there is nothing too big or too small to bring before our God in prayer. Scripture commands, "Cast all your cares upon Him, because He cares for you." As Augustine of Hippo put it nearly two millennia ago, God is "closer to us than we are to ourselves." We pray to a God who listens. We worship a God who cares.

Later in the evening, during that first meeting with Scott, we sat together for dinner and encouraged each other with conversation about our faith and God's faithfulness in our lives across the years, and across continents. God's grace through conversations like that one has sustained my faith "through many dangers, toils, and snares." Scott's friendship has been a true blessing in my life.

As a man of strong faith and integrity, deeply committed to family, he calls us back, as he did in his inaugural speech to Parliament, to what Abraham Lincoln called his greatest concern—"not whether God is on our side" but "to be on God's side, for God is always right." This we can only hope to achieve with the help of God, sought in prayer. So help us God.

My great hope is that you would find encouragement in this task through Scott's inspiring story in the pages of this book, much as I have been encouraged by Scott through that first meeting and our conversations since. May his words of hope point you ever beyond a prime minister and politician to the goodness and faithfulness of God and the object of our hope, the Lord Jesus Christ.

—Mike Pence, 48th Vice President of the United States

PREFACE

"For I know the plans I have for you," says the
LORD. "They are plans for good and not for
disaster, to give you a future and a hope."
JEREMIAH 29:11 (NLT)

President Truman is rumored to have said, "If you want a friend in Washington, get a dog." There's no actual record of him ever saying it, but as a politician who has spent more than twenty years in the business, including at the highest level, I can tell you it's still good advice. Winston Churchill also seemed to think so, saying, "If you don't love my dog, you . . . can't love me."[1]

My dog's name is Buddy. He lives with me; my wife, Jen; and our two teenage daughters. Jen and I have been married for over thirty years. We were high school sweethearts and have lived almost our entire lives together. We also have a cat named Charlie—he's the boss.

We live in Australia in a place called "the Shire." There are no hobbits or tiny houses carved into the hillside, like in Tolkien's *The Lord of the Rings*. The Shire is a beautiful group of beachside suburbs in southern Sydney, with gum trees (eucalyptus) lining the streets. The Shire is the kind of place you never want to leave. It's where our children, Abbey and Lily, were born; where we go to church as a family; where I support my local rugby league team, the Sharks; and where I walk Buddy along the beach. It was this community that first elected me to Australia's national parliament in 2007. We love it here.

Being a family member of a politician is not easy. Former Australian prime minister Tony Abbott is known for saying, "As politicians, we are volunteers, but our families are conscripts." It's true. Our girls were born into this life and know no other. And my wife, Jen, has shouldered the majority of the parenting load due to my constant absences. So, in mid-2018, when I was federal treasurer and had already served five years as a senior cabinet minister, Jen and the girls decided they wanted a puppy. Abbey had just turned eleven, and Lily was nine years old. Jen found a dog breeder through Instagram, and we pored over the images of puppy litters. They were all too cute for words. Looking out through the paws of his siblings in one image was a tiny newborn black schnoodle (a cross between a schnauzer and a poodle). He had deep, dark eyes and a crumpled little face. That was the one.

Over the next few months, we watched Buddy's progress online as he got ready to come and live with us. We were all very excited. When the day finally came to pick up Buddy, we jumped in the car and made the four-hour drive to the country, where he was waiting.

We all knew that getting a puppy was not going to change the challenges and pressures we faced as a family in public office. However, the minute we saw Buddy, it was love at first sight for all of us. Those deep, dark eyes that had originally captured us stared up from his thick, black, furry face as if to say, "Let's go home."

Just a few weeks later, in a surprising plot twist, I unexpectedly became Australia's thirtieth prime minister (PM). I would go on to serve for almost four years during one of the most challenging periods any prime minister has encountered in our country since the Second World War.

We endured drought, floods, bushfires, cyclones, the global COVID-19 pandemic, a global and domestic recession, and even a plague of mice. On top of this, we contended with an aggressive Chinese communist regime trying to bully Australia, our region, and the world. We saw the end of our longest war in Afghanistan and the start of a new one in Ukraine. Despite the historic challenges we faced during my time as prime minister, Australia came through it all exceptionally well. A day rarely passes when someone doesn't come up to me to share a quiet "thank you" for leading Australia through.

Looking back on that trip into the country, we were so blessed to have Buddy come into our home just when he did. We had no idea our family was about to come under more strain than we ever could have imagined. The challenges and difficult decisions I faced in the unknown of a global pandemic that threatened the lives and livelihoods of millions of Australians daily were often overwhelming and always exhausting. Every day there was a new challenge and a new threat requiring another new solution. Decisions often had to be made in minutes. There were also the relentless, often cruel political attacks and media coverage that are the drumbeat of a politician's life—never more painful than when it included attacks on Jen and the girls, especially on social media.

Through all of these challenges, Buddy was our constant companion, always there for a pat when you walked in the door or to lay his head on Jen's lap when she needed cheering up or just some company during the times I was called away. When he came to visit me at the prime minister's residence in Canberra, called "The

Lodge," we would walk around the grounds together. Buddy did his small part in helping us get through the most turbulent time we'd experienced as a family. He has now grown out of his crumpled puppy face but remains an important part of our family. And, yes, so does Charlie, for all the cat lovers.

You may be thinking as you read this, *Wasn't this guy the prime minister of a country? Why is he telling me about his dog?* It seems like such a small thing. Surely there were bigger things going on that I should be talking about. You're right. There were bigger things, and we'll get to those. But there is nothing bigger than truly understanding the importance of God's presence and promises in our lives—and God cares about the small details, such as bringing Buddy into our lives at just the right time, as much as He does about the big things, like sustaining Australia through a global pandemic. In Jeremiah 29:11, God says, "For I know the plans I have for you. . . . They are plans for good and not for disaster, to give you a future and a hope" (NLT). In the more ordinary language of The Message, it says, "I know what I'm doing. I have it all planned out—plans to take care of you, not abandon you, plans to give you the future you hope for." When God talks about His plans for our good, it's not just the big stuff He's interested in. Sure, Buddy was just a puppy, and lots of people have dogs. But so many of God's plans for our good are in the smallest details of our lives.

We also find God's goodness in more than just the good times and the big achievements. Oftentimes we experience it right in the fierceness of the storm. In all of life's circumstances—positive and negative, hopeful and hopeless—God's goodness is the anchor that holds. And the greatest of all our blessings is the hope He holds for us in eternity (Ephesians 1:18). The key is to look at life through the prism of God's goodness, knowing that His plans are for your good.

I have won. I have lost. I have succeeded. I have failed. I have been right. I have been wrong. I have visited with royalty in their palaces and dined with presidents and prime ministers. I have sat in the dust and poverty of central Australia with Aboriginal Australians and with Rohingya families in their desperate refugee camps in Myanmar. I have been honored and derided. I have been praised and ridiculed. I have known deep sorrow, anger, and humiliation. I have known love, joy, and friendship.

In all of life's circumstances—positive and negative, hopeful and hopeless—God's goodness is the anchor that holds.

Most politicians write books about what they've done. This book is my story of what I believe God has done for me through His faithfulness in all my life's circumstances and how I came to truly understand God's promise in Jeremiah 29:11. It's also a book about what God can do in your life. His promise is not just for me, and it's not just for good times. It's for you and whatever you're facing today too.

In Genesis 32:24 we read how Jacob wrestled with a man of God for an entire night. It was pretty weird. In this book I reveal my own wrestling with God about the big questions of life that we all contend with: Who am I? How should I live? What should I hope for? I don't have all the answers. I am still on the journey. The thoughts I present here are the product of prayer, meditating on God's Word, the counsel of Christian friends, the teaching of pastors over the years, and just seeking to live out my faith. I pray God will bless and transform you as you wrestle with these same questions in your own life.

In 1873 Fanny Crosby wrote the hymn "Blessed Assurance." It has been a favorite of mine for many years. Every time I recall it, I can hear my mother-in-law, Beth, harmonizing above the chorus. It is the third verse I love most:

> *Perfect submission, all is at rest*
> *I in my Savior am happy and blessed*
> *Watching and waiting, looking above,*
> *Filled with His goodness, lost in His love.*[2]

The refrain goes on to say, "This is my story, this is my song, / praising my Savior all the day long." That is what this book is really all about.

In Australia, and especially in the Shire, when we want to say how excited or happy we are about something or someone, we turn it into a rhetorical question. We might say, "How good are the Sharks?" after my local National Rugby League team has had a great win, or "How good is Jen?" or just "How good?" When we won the miracle election in 2019, I became famous for saying on that night, "How good is Australia?" Well, "How good is God?" sums up how I feel about His impact on my life. It is a question God answers positively for me every day.

Like you, I'm far from perfect. I can't pretend to have lived a life unstained by sin, selfishness, pride, and more. After all, I'm a politician! But I can testify to a life eternally marked by God's goodness, by His saving grace through Jesus Christ, and by the sustaining presence of His Holy Spirit. My prayer is that He will give you eyes to see that His plans are for your good too.

Part One

WHO AM I?

Discovering Your Purpose

To live a life of blessing, you need to really
know who you are and what you're about.

Chapter One

WHAT DO YOU BELIEVE?

I am not ashamed, for I know whom I have believed,
and I am convinced that [God] is able to protect
what I have entrusted to Him until that day.
2 TIMOTHY 1:12

I cleared most of the people out of my study who had joined me at the prime minister's official residence at Kirribilli House overlooking Sydney Harbour. It was election night in Australia: Saturday, May 21, 2022. While the opposition had not yet won the necessary seats in Parliament to form a government, I had been through enough elections to know where things were heading. There were practical things I now needed to arrange, so I asked my most senior staff to stay while everyone else joined our other guests in the sitting room.

I was disappointed with the looming outcome of this election. I had worked hard and campaigned well. I had trusted God and put everything I had into the job. It was over. It was a hard loss. We had been soundly defeated. We had all sat in this same room three years earlier when we realized we had won an extraordinary and unlikely victory. A miracle victory, I called it. That's politics: some days you win, some days you lose.

Over the next few days I would formally tender my resignation as prime minister to the governor-general. After three terms, and almost nine years, the government of one of the world's oldest and most prosperous democracies would peacefully change hands once again. On the other side of the world, in Ukraine, a much younger democracy was fighting for its survival against an illegal Russian invasion. Perspective is important at times like this.

After speaking with my wife, Jen, I went upstairs to tell our daughters, Abbey and Lily. They had come to live at the prime minister's residence from our home in the Shire as little girls and would now be leaving as teenagers. On nights like this they often liked to keep to themselves. As sisters they had been through a unique experience together. The house was full. Our family, friends, and staff had gathered, so the girls had retreated to the privacy and quiet of Abbey's bedroom upstairs. They were sitting together on Abbey's bed. I sat down on the other end and just looked at them for a moment. These were my miracle girls, God's great gift to me and Jen. I was looking into the faces of God's goodness. Life's most bitter disappointments don't stand a chance when you're confronted with the truth of God's blessings in your life. It was just what I needed.

> Life's most bitter disappointments don't stand a chance when you're confronted with the truth of God's blessings in your life.

I told them, "Girls, Dad has lost the election, and I won't be prime minister anymore . . . we're going home." They knew I was disappointed. "I gave it everything I had, girls," I said, but they already knew that. They both cried, not because we had lost but just because they loved their dad and didn't like to see me disappointed. They had been on this journey with me far more than I had ever really appreciated. They saw, even when I was away, how much this job had impacted me and commanded every minute of every day. They knew just how much I had put into it. Jen would tell me they always knew when the job was getting me down or when I was under intense stress. They could sense it. I always tried to hide it from them, but they knew. That night, they gave me a hug that only daughters know how to give their dad.

Despite the genuine disappointment of losing, I also felt a strange calm. Leading our country had been a great privilege, and I wanted to continue to serve. However, leading my country through a global pandemic, natural disasters, constant security threats, and recession in a malevolent and often toxic political environment had taken a heavy toll. It had been an extraordinary time. I don't believe any prime minister in Australia had seen a time like it since the Second World War and the Great Depression. Two prime ministers who led Australia during those times had died in office. After almost four years in the top job, nine years in cabinet, and having just completed a second national election campaign, I was exhausted, physically and emotionally.

That night I remembered a conversation I'd had almost nine years before. It was just before the 2013 election. We were feeling confident of victory after six years as the opposition party. I took the time to get a few words of wisdom from one of my mentors. Peter Costello was not just a successful former cabinet minister and Australia's longest-serving federal treasurer; he also shares my Christian faith. After we had finished our coffee, I walked with him onto Collins Street in Melbourne. As we went to cross the road, Peter turned to me and said, "And another thing, Scott. Don't waste a day. It goes really fast." I would learn he was right. As I looked back over nearly nine years, I took comfort in the fact that I knew I had taken his advice.

Defeat is a place many know well. It can be lonely. A place of questioning, fear, doubt, and even despair. Our defeats can be small or great. They can be experienced in the full humiliating light of public display or in the private agony of disappointed hope. Our defeats can accumulate and compound. The burden can grow heavy and weigh us down. Defeat can suffocate us, blind us, immobilize us. It can leave us cold and numb. Bitterness often accompanies defeat and spawns self-pity, jealousy, grievances, and vindictiveness.

Sure, you may feel these things, and such feelings are natural. You may also have every right to feel the way you do. You may have been treated unfairly or awfully betrayed. But while the Bible refers to righteous anger, you won't find any mention of righteous bitterness. What I read about in the Bible is a gospel of grace, love, and forgiveness. We all deal with disappointments in life, but regardless of their cause, bitterness is not the answer. Bitterness is not what you want controlling your life's path. Jesus showed us a better way. In politics I regularly saw bitterness destroy people's lives. In politics there are rarely happy endings. Few succeed in the way they hoped to. Even those who do succeed still grow bitter, unable to get over being deprived of the office they once held and invested so much of their identity and self-worth in.

Faith does not make you immune to defeat, but our faith in God as followers of Jesus does enable us to deal with it.

At times of defeat, what you believe really matters. What have you really built your life on? Where does your hope truly reside? Where does your love and affection ultimately rest? Disappointment and defeat will reveal these things. Faith does not make you immune to defeat, but our faith in God as followers of Jesus does enable us to deal with it. God has a different perspective on what we call defeat. This is what I believe the apostle Paul meant when he told the church in Rome that we are "more than conquerors" (Romans 8:37 NIV). As Christians we can always know victory through Christ, even in defeat. Jesus did.

AFTER DEFEAT

The prime minister's official vehicle is a white, armor-plated BMW 7 Series with the number plate C1, which stands for Commonwealth One. I rang the leader of the opposition and congratulated him on his victory as Jen and I left Kirribilli House together in C1 for the last time. The Australian flag on the hood was flapping in the night air on the way to the hotel where our party supporters had gathered in the ballroom. The trip takes about fifteen minutes. We drove across Sydney's famous Harbour Bridge, looking out over an illuminated Sydney Opera House. We felt privileged that we had been able to do what we had done. Our overwhelming feeling was just one of gratitude. Three years before, we had humbly welcomed victory. Tonight, we would be dignified in accepting defeat. I thanked our supporters and encouraged them to keep their heads high because we had left the country stronger than we had found it. Importantly, we had seen Australia through the great storm of the pandemic.

The next morning we headed, as a family, to our home church in the Shire—Horizon Church. Our pastor invited me up to the platform to say a few words. I hadn't planned on doing this. It was a spur-of-the-moment thing.

The congregation gave me a warm reception as I walked to the platform. I was genuinely grateful for their support and that of hundreds of thousands, if not millions, of other Christians around the country who had prayed for me and my family constantly during my time as prime minister. I know many still do.

I thanked my church for their prayers and support and said it had been a very difficult walk for me and our family while I was PM. Invoking the famous passage in Esther 4:14, I believed I had served "for such a time as this," and it was now "such as time as that." I believed this time had now passed. I said, "God calls us, if you are a prime minister, pastor, running a business, teaching in schools, working in the police force. It doesn't matter. We are called to trust and obey. That is the life of faithfulness. We live our faith each and every day."

I then turned to share a passage in Habakkuk 3:17–18. I had to stop to regain my composure, as the words would not come out of my mouth. There were tears, but not of sadness. They were the tears of being overwhelmed by the assurance of God and the hope and trust we can have in Him as Christians. I struggled through the passage:

> Even if the fig tree does not blossom,
> And there is no fruit on the vines,
> If the yield of the olive fails,
> And the fields produce no food,
> Even if the flock disappears from the fold,
> And there are no cattle in the stalls,
> Yet I will triumph in the LORD,
> I will rejoice in the God of my salvation.

Deep down I knew that although this season may have ended, a new one would certainly begin. I finished my remarks quoting Micah 7:7–8:

But as for me, I will be on the watch for the LORD;

I will wait for the God of my salvation.

My God will hear me.

Do not rejoice over me, enemy of mine.

Though I fall I will rise;

Though I live in darkness, the LORD is a light for me.

Those were the last public words I would speak as prime minister. I was pleased they were His words and in His house.

I had come to terms with our defeat. I respected the judgment of the Australian people. All things come to an end. I was not angry at God. Why should I be? He was still with me. His blessing is not found in the achievement; it is found in His presence. However, I was not prepared for what happened next. I had expected the political caravan to move on and that my family and I would now be able to catch our breath and also move on, with dignity and respect. That didn't happen.

> *His blessing is not found in the achievement; it is found in His presence.*

After I lost the election, my opponents were not content to leave it there. In Australian politics we call this a "pile on." Not satisfied with my defeat, they engaged in a campaign to humiliate, discredit, and cancel me. It was graceless, brutal, and it hurt.

When you're in the job, you are so busy dealing with the numerous issues you must contend with that there is often little time to truly absorb the personal attacks that come your way. You develop a thick skin. In these days of social media, the attacks are far more sophisticated and effective. They create a cycle of hate that distorts reality. I never really recognized how vicious the attacks on me were until after I left office. Once the music stops, the attacks can be all you see and hear, even when you try to ignore them. As Christians we know what principalities and powers are often behind these attacks (Ephesians 6:12). I decided not to take the bait, as I believed it would have only made matters worse. I turned down interviews and turned the other cheek. I knew that what was being said did not represent the truth of who I was, what I was about, and what we had been able to achieve. Wherever I went, people continued to approach me to say thank you for what we had done for them during the pandemic and my time as prime minister. This was in stark contrast to the public narrative now being driven by my political opponents and some in the media.

I also believed that my response was how a former prime minister should behave. While my opponents wanted to keep kicking, I wanted to follow the dignified example of those who had left office quietly and moved on. I recall that during the pandemic our first female prime minister, Julia Gillard, was being baited by the media into being critical of me and my government. Perhaps they thought that because she was from the other side of politics she would take a swipe. She refused to be drawn. She showed a lot of class. I hope to follow her example. But the ongoing attacks were making it difficult to adjust to post-prime ministerial life. I was uninterested in going back and seemingly unable to move forward.

WHERE ARE YOU, GOD?

I like to pray out loud, but only when I'm on my own. I do it in the car or when I'm out walking or sitting somewhere alone. I recommend it. When you say things out loud, they take on a greater significance. Thoughts and feelings become expressions and declarations, and you really start to own and clarify the way you truly think and feel.

During these months I had plenty of these conversations with God. I would take Buddy for long walks where I would listen to audiobooks, podcasts, and sermons and just pray to God. Things got pretty heated between me and God as I poured my heart out. *Why are You letting my enemies get the better of me? Why are my prayers going unanswered? Why have You raised me up only to see me now crushed and humiliated?*

In Psalm 35, David prayed a similar prayer: "Lord, how long will You look on? Rescue my soul from their ravages. . . . You have seen it, LORD, do not keep silent; Lord, do not be far from me. Stir Yourself, and awake to my right and to my cause, my God and my Lord" (verses 17, 22–23).

You have probably also felt like this at some point, demanding an answer: *Why don't my children listen to me? Why does my husband constantly fail to get it? Why is my marriage failing? Why does everything have to be such a struggle, Lord?*

My prayer would continue, *As best as I can determine, I am seeking to follow You and live a faithful life, Lord. I know I'm not perfect and can't do this in my own strength, and I'm not trying to. That's why I'm looking to You. I pray, I read Your Word, I worship You, and I confess You. I've read Your psalms; I've read Your promises in Isaiah and Jeremiah. Why don't these seem to apply to me? Where are You, God?*

Rather than judging and rebuking me for my outburst, God turned my mind to Jesus. I sensed His response in my spirit.

So Scott, your enemies are getting the better of you, are they? You think you have been unfairly treated, have you? You're being humiliated and mocked? People are lying about you and misrepresenting you? You may have heard about some of My experiences. My friends deserted Me when I needed them most. My people lied about Me and believed the lies told about Me. Even in My own hometown they rejected Me. I was betrayed by one of My closest friends. The rest of them just ran off, and one of them even said he never knew Me. My people welcomed Me with praises into Jerusalem, lining up all week for Me to heal them and teach them. Yet by the end of the week, they wanted Me crucified. When given the choice between saving a murderer and Me, they chose the murderer! The authorities who sat in judgment over Me chose to placate the noisy mob rather than do what was right and just. When they nailed Me to a cross where I suffered and died, even My own Father in heaven had to look away.

Scott, I get it. I've been there and worse, and you know what? I did it all for you, because I really love you. I've walked this path, Scott. I can show you how to move forward from here. Just follow Me. Just believe in Me and trust Me.

Now that's a comeback! My experience cannot be equated with Jesus'. It stopped me in my tracks.

THE COST OF BELIEF

Having faith in God as a Christian is not easy. Having faith as a Christian comes at a price. Anything that really matters always does.

In almost every suburb and town across Australia you will find a memorial to those in their community who lost their lives in the service of our country in our defense forces. The greatest of our Australian memorials is the National War Memorial in Canberra, where just over one hundred thousand names are inscribed. Your name doesn't go on that wall unless you paid the ultimate price.

One name on that wall is Sergeant Brett Till. In 2009 Brett was killed by an improvised explosive device while on deployment in Afghanistan. He had two young children and a third on the way with his lovely young wife, Bree. Brett and his family lived in the Shire. Brett and Bree's then unborn son would later go to school with my youngest daughter, Lily.

Forty-one Australians serving in Afghanistan were killed in our longest ever conflict. Brett was the ninth to be killed. When I offered my own tribute to Brett in Parliament, it hit home hard. Here was someone from my own community with a full life of fatherhood, service, and love ahead of him. All of this had been taken in an instant. His family and all those who loved him would forever have a hole in their lives that could never be filled. It made me think of previous conflicts where such horrific and numerous losses were a daily occurrence. The cost of this is impossible to account.

I was prime minister when our involvement in the war in Afghanistan came to an end. I was in Perth when I was formally advised of the final withdrawal of US troops by the US president, which we had been expecting. I stood in front of the media to make the announcement. It was difficult to find the words, so I simply just fought back the tears and read the names of those we had lost, pausing over Brett's, and reflected on the terrible cost.

Soon after I would be overseeing the final phases of our evacuation from Kabul. Things had deteriorated quickly. The Taliban was closing in on the city faster than intelligence had predicted. We had already withdrawn the vast majority of our people some months in advance, anticipating that the final phase was likely to be quite chaotic. During this time we were working to bring as many Afghans as possible, who had assisted our defense forces in Afghanistan, and their families, to Australia.

We had now reached the final days. The Taliban was taking over. It was becoming increasingly dangerous for all those involved, whether processing visas on the tarmac or flying the missions in and out of Kabul. The clock was now running to get everyone out before the Taliban took over the airport. For ten days we had met constantly to plan and execute the evacuation of as many people as we could. At the start of this operation we had estimated an airlift of nine hundred people. We ended up evacuating four thousand.

On the final day of our operation, we had filled the final plane. This included all our own people who had been running the ground operation. It was now their turn to be evacuated. They would be the last to leave. It was time for wheels up. I was in the middle of chairing a cabinet meeting when I was asked to take a call from the chief of the defense force (CDF), General Angus Campbell, who advised me that a young mother who was approved for evacuation had managed to fight her way through the crowds with her child to the Abbey Gate on the far side of the airport perimeter. Rescuing them would mean delaying departure of our final flight and having our troops undertake a dangerous mission of around one and a half kilometers each way to pick them up and escort them to the plane.

The situation at the Abbey Gate had completely deteriorated. There were people everywhere in the most terrible and desperate conditions. Obtaining slots on the runway for takeoff was also a problem. Our final slot was now—take it or leave it. We didn't have another one. You can imagine how many planes were trying to get out. The situation on the ground was becoming more dangerous by the minute. If we did not go now, we did not know how long we would have to wait to get our people out, nor what could potentially happen while we waited. I gave the go-ahead to rescue the mother and her young child and for our plane to pull off the runway onto the stand. I prayed quietly to myself. It was a nerve-racking wait. I cannot remember how long it was before the CDF called again to report back, but it seemed like an eternity. He called to let me know that the escort had been successful and that everyone was safely on board. The mother and her child had been rescued. I instructed the CDF to take off as soon as they could. After a further nervous wait, we were able to secure another slot, and the flight made it to safety in Dubai. I later learned that when the mother and her child boarded the aircraft, all the passengers cheered.

Within just a few hours of that final rescue a suicide bomber made his way to the Abbey Gate where he detonated his deadly payload, taking the lives of thirteen young US service members and numerous Afghans lined up at the gate and maiming many others.

Those who served in Afghanistan were heroes. For too many the war claimed their lives. Others would survive only to wrestle with the mental and physical scars of war. Their service came at a great price. Freedom is never free. If you believe in something, there is always a price.

In Hebrews we read about the great heroes of the Christian faith. It reads like a kind of honor roll that we see on war memorials, detailing the achievements and the cost of their faith. "By faith [they] conquered kingdoms, performed acts of righteousness, . . . shut the mouths of lions, quenched the power of fire, escaped the edge of the sword, . . . put foreign armies to flight" (Hebrews 11:33–34). But then we read they "experienced mocking and flogging, and further, chains and imprisonment. They were stoned, they were sawn in two, . . . put to death with the sword; they went about . . . being destitute, afflicted, tormented" (Hebrews 11:36–37).

If you want the type of faith that will anchor you in a storm . . . it will cost you.

If you want the type of faith that will anchor you in a storm, that will enable you to see blessing in times of defeat and find the way forward when nothing seems clear, it will cost you.

Abraham understood this. He had grown up in a place called Ur. This was a thriving port city, the London, New York, or Shanghai of its time. Abraham was seventy years old and likely living a prosperous and successful life when out of nowhere God told him to pack up his things and leave, "not knowing where he was going" (Hebrews 11:8).

Belief meant obedience for Abraham. What is the point of saying you believe in something if you are not prepared to act on it? That's not belief. That's just an opinion. I learned in leadership that plenty of people have opinions but only a few make decisions and take action. For that to happen, belief is required.

No doubt Abraham had all sorts of plans for his life in Ur. But God came and disrupted them. He told Abraham to leave all this behind and go somewhere else. Belief meant surrendering his own plans to those God had for him. It meant embracing all the uncertainty this entailed. It meant truly accepting and trusting in what God had for Abraham over what he hoped to achieve for himself.

We can be control freaks. We think to ourselves, *Sure, I believe, but I want God to realize* my *plans*. Such plans may not be selfish. They may even be plans for Christian ministry or service. Ironically, we sometimes think we have a better plan to serve God than He does for us.

Abraham's story didn't end there, of course. God told Abraham to look up into the night sky, and He promised him that his descendants would be as numerous as the stars (Genesis 26:4). God promised Abraham that his wife, Sarah, would have a son. Just one problem: Sarah was well past the age for having children. God was promising Abraham the impossible.

Paul tells us that Abraham responded "in hope against hope," "not waver[ing] in unbelief," and "being fully assured that what God had promised, He was able also to perform" (Romans 4:18–22). Abraham really believed that God would do what He promised. He believed that God would make the impossible possible, and that's just what He did. Fast-forward and we find Abraham and

Sarah's son, Isaac, now growing up. A living miracle. We then read in Genesis 22:2 that God said to Abraham, "Take now your son, your only son, whom you love, Isaac, . . . and offer him there as a burnt offering." Whaaaat?! That certainly wasn't mentioned in God's "starry, starry night" chat with Abraham. How do you begin to get your head around what God just asked Abraham to do? Abraham didn't even seem to try.

We can waste years torturing ourselves trying to make sense of what God is doing in our lives. Abraham just obeyed. He knew that faith meant obedience. Sometimes we may live to see the purpose. Sometimes we are just blindly sowing the seed for another generation to harvest. That's how God works. He is not bound by our mortal time frames, convenience, or comprehension. He is the great "I AM" (Exodus 3:14–16).

Abraham never lost sight of the Source of his blessing. He had decided long ago to leave Ur and follow God's plan, not his own. He understood that whatever had come his way, it had come because of God's blessing to him and by trusting God through obedience. He understood, in reverence, that he had no right to tell God what He could do with the blessings He had provided to him. His role was to trust and obey. So Abraham just got up early in the morning, saddled his donkey, took two of his young men with him and his son Isaac, split wood for the burnt offering, and went to the place where God had told him to go. Wow!

Before you think that Abraham was a callous father with no regard for his son's well-being, notice what he said next. When it was time for Abraham and Isaac to walk the final stage of their journey together, Abraham said to those traveling with him, "Stay here with the donkey, and I and the boy will go over there; *and we will worship and return to you*" (Genesis 22:5, emphasis added). Abraham had every intention of following through on what God had asked him to do in offering up Isaac, but at the same time he told those traveling with them that they would both be back. It doesn't make any sense. How do you square that circle? In Hebrews 11:19 we find the answer: Abraham "considered that God is able to raise people even from the dead."

Abraham was not just promised a son. He was promised descendants through his son. And not just any son, but the son born to Sarah. God was quite specific. He said of Sarah, "I will bless her, and she shall be a mother of nations; kings of peoples will come from her" (Genesis 17:16). Abraham believed this promise, and he knew God was faithful to His promises. This had been his life's experience. No matter what, Abraham believed that God would find a way for His promise to be established through Isaac. If that meant raising Isaac from the dead, that is what God would do, and Isaac would be coming back with Abraham to where they left the donkey with the others.

The rest of the story we know. Having tested Abraham's faith, God stayed his hand and provided a ram in the bushes that was offered as the sacrifice in Isaac's place. God's promise was then fulfilled through Isaac. When God first promised Abraham that his descendants would be as the stars of the heavens, He knew how Abraham would be tested. He knew the struggles and frustrations Abraham and

> *We must obey and commit ourselves to God's plan, not our own.*

Sarah would go through and the mistakes they would make. But His promises would always remain.

The path of our future is known only to God. We have the joy of being able to look back over our lives and see the testaments to His goodness. As for what lies ahead, we can only trust and obey, because that's what true faith does.

As I write this book, my future remains uncertain. Maybe you're also in the middle of transition, uncertainty, anxiety, doubt. Maybe you've been talking to God and feel like you haven't heard back.

I hope that maybe you hear an echo of His answer to you through His answer to me. He's got this. His plans are for our good, not our harm, to give us a future and a hope. That's more than enough. We just have to believe in Him and trust Him. Like Abraham, the only way to live is by faith. Like Abraham, we must obey and commit ourselves to God's plan, not our own.

Chapter Two

WHAT ARE YOU GOING TO DO?

The LORD said to Moses, "Why are you crying out to
Me? Tell the sons of Israel to go forward. As for you,
lift up your staff and reach out with your hand."
EXODUS 14:15–16

So, there's Moses standing in the middle of hundreds of thousands of desperate and terrified people who had trusted him
to take them out of Egypt. Behind him is Pharaoh's army, rapidly
closing in. In front of him is the Red Sea, blocking his escape.

Moses had seen God do the impossible before. He was convinced
of God's plan to bring the people of Israel out of slavery and take
them to the promised land. Even in this desperate situation, he did
not surrender to the doubts consuming those around him. This was
the act of a strong leader who had confidence in the purposes and
plans of God.

So Moses stood firm, assuring the people of Israel that the Lord's salvation was at hand. "The LORD will fight for you," he declared (Exodus 14:14). What a strong statement of faith. But then God says to Moses, "Why are you crying out to Me?" (Exodus 14:15). Say what?!

Surely, when faced with such a hopeless situation, it is understandable for us to raise our cries to God. This hardly seems unreasonable, let alone a reason for Moses to be rebuked by God. I mean, cut Moses some slack. Can't you see the situation he's dealing with here, God, and especially after Moses had just so confidently declared his faith and confidence in You for their salvation? Come on, God, get behind the guy. He's doing his best for You, after all.

Surely now was the time for God to just show up and blow the Egyptians away with some good Old Testament smiting. But that's not what happened. God's instructions for the people were to "go forward" (Exodus 14:15). And to Moses God said, "As for you, lift up your staff and reach out with your hand" (Exodus 14:16).

Of course God could have parted the Red Sea without Moses lifting a finger and the people of Israel just sitting there by the shore, but that's not what immediately happened. No, in order for this salvation to be realized, God first required something from both Moses and the people of Israel. They had to take the first step.

Moses's declaration of faith was not enough—nor were his cries. God wanted Moses to act on his faith, and He wanted the same from the people of Israel. They had to get up and go forward, not passively wait for deliverance. As for Moses, he had to pick up his staff and stretch out his hand.

This was the same staff Moses threw to the ground when he encountered God in front of the burning bush, the same staff that God turned into a snake and then back into a staff again. The same staff God had used to demonstrate His power before Pharaoh.

The same staff that would later strike the rock in the wilderness to draw forth water. But there was nothing particularly special about Moses's staff.

For a generation Moses had been wandering around Midian herding his father-in-law's flocks with this staff. I suspect Moses liked his staff. It was probably very familiar to him, just like my favorite cap is to me. Let me tell you about my cap.

The first thing I did after becoming prime minister was to visit a fifth-generation outback sheep station, or ranch as they are known in the United States, called Bunginderry. It was located near a little town in South West Queensland called Quilpie, which has a population of just over 650 people.

I went there with my deputy prime minister and good friend, Michael McCormack (I call him the Big Mac). We went to see firsthand the terrible impact of the long drought that Australia was suffering through and to stand with our hurting rural communities as we worked to find ways to provide further help.

Now, I was a boy from the suburbs of Sydney. I was not from the bush and certainly not the outback. When you go to the outback, it's a smart thing to wear a hat. It gets pretty hot out there (over 100 degrees Fahrenheit). Oftentimes when city politicians go to the outback, they wear what's called an Akubra. It's a wide-brimmed felt hat that the stockmen and farmers wear. In the United States it would be a Stetson or some other type of "cowboy" hat.

I had dutifully brought along my own Akubra. But I also had stuffed in my bag my surf cap, which I wear at home in the Shire. I turned to my parliamentary colleague, Scotty Buchholz, who was on the trip with me. Scotty is a very big man and a real Queenslander. I said to him before we got off the plane, "Mate, I really don't feel comfortable wearing this Akubra. I'm not a farmer. I look like a complete poser."

Scotty readily agreed. "You do look like a *bleeping* poser, mate." He has never been one to mince his words. He said, "Well, what else have you got? You'll need a *bleeping* hat, mate." I showed him my surf cap, and he said, "That'll do, mate. People just expect you to be yourself up here. And that's who you are. So put your *bleeping* hat on and get goin' because you can't be *bleeping* late." It was great advice, albeit colorfully put, as Scotty has a way of doing.

The Tully family was fighting their way through a sixth year of drought. I will never forget their strength and optimism. I looked out at the paddock near the homestead, and it was a dust bowl. Sometimes our lives can feel like that. Stephen Tully pulled out a photo of the same paddock taken before the drought that showed grass growing up to the knees. He told me with a great sense of optimism and determination that it would be back. When he looked at the dryness of that paddock, he would also look at the photo and remind himself why it was so important to press on.

After showing me around their property, sharing his experiences with me, and introducing me to the family, including the dogs, Stephen saw my cap and decided I needed a better one to mark the occasion. It's a dark navy blue cap, with a big red *B* on the front, which stands for Bunginderry. It looks a bit like a Boston Red Sox cap. I love that cap. It is a constant reminder of the tremendous resilience and optimism of the Australian people, like the Tullys. I wore it often as PM, and I still do today. After that visit, people gave me a cap everywhere I went around the country. I have hundreds of them now. But the cap Stephen gave me will always be my favorite.

Anyway, back to Moses and his staff.

I can see Moses asking his wife, Zipporah, about his staff, just like I ask Jen, "Do you know where my cap is?" "Zipporah," he would cry out, "I can't find my staff. Where did you put it?" "What, again?" she'd probably reply. "I was sure I left it by the bed," Moses might say in complete disbelief, walking aimlessly around in circles (as men do). Wisely not buying into the oft-repeated allegation that Zipporah was somehow responsible for Moses's inability to find his own staff, she would decide to just be helpful, knowing the sooner he finds this thing, the better off everyone will be (you may be getting the sense I am projecting a bit here). "Perhaps you left it at Dad's place," Zipporah might have helpfully suggested, "when you were over there last night talking about whatever you two talk about." Moses would then trudge over to his father-in-law's tent, finding his elusive staff, and off he would go, able to face the day.

So here he is, standing before the Red Sea, and God says, "See that staff I put in your hand? Raise it up." God wanted Moses to use what He had put in his hand to accomplish His purposes on this day, as he had done on so many occasions before. God then tells Moses to divide the sea! What? Say that again. That's right, God wanted Moses to divide an actual

> *Whatever God has given us through life's experiences, He wants us to bring it and trust Him with what happens next.*

sea. God doesn't say, "Reach out your hand and I will divide the sea." God says, "Reach out with your hand over the sea and divide it" (Exodus 14:16).

Now, I know we read a bit later that after Moses had reached out his hand, "the LORD swept the sea back by a strong east wind all night, and turned the sea into dry land, and the waters were divided" (Exodus 14:21). But that is not what God said at the start. He told Moses to stretch out his hand and divide the sea. Next time you think God is asking you to do something that you believe is beyond you, just remember that God asked Moses to part a sea. Nothing is impossible with God (Luke 1:37).

We can believe. We can cry out to God, but God wants us to do more. He wants us to act on our faith. He wants us to take the initiative, to pick up what He has put in our hand—our talents, our experiences, our energies, our resources, our networks—and let Him work in us to achieve His plans and purposes. Whatever God has given us through life's experiences, He wants us to bring it and trust Him with what happens next. He wants us to raise it up, spread forth our hand, and then see what He can do. What happens after that is up to God.

"I'VE ALWAYS BELIEVED IN MIRACLES"

Shortly after 7:00 a.m. on the day I became Australia's thirtieth prime minister, I sent a text message to a group of pastor friends saying, "Staff is up, I am walking toward the sea."

My message to my pastor friends was not a vain proclamation that God was going to "anoint" me to the role of prime minister. Nor would I dare to make any comparison between me and Moses. It was just making a statement of practical faith—that I was taking action, stepping forward, and trusting God with whatever happened next.

On that day, it was not clear how things would play out. At the time, my party was in power and I was a senior member of the government. But the PM was facing pressure from within our party. In Australia, our parliamentary system allows a sitting prime minister to be removed by his own party members in Parliament and a new leader elected by a vote of those same members. This had already happened to prime ministers from both sides of Australian politics on four occasions during the past ten years. Over the weekend there had been some reports that there might be an attempt to remove the sitting prime minister, Malcolm Turnbull, that week. I had been Malcolm's friend for many years. He had appointed me as his treasurer when he became prime minister, and we had achieved a lot together.

Leadership rumors in parliamentary politics happen from time to time, and the media revel in it. But sometimes those rumors turn out to be true. My own inquiries about the reports led me to conclude it was nothing more than the usual idle speculation. I had relayed that to the PM over the weekend. He asked whether he should try and flush out any challengers during the next parliamentary sitting week by calling on a vote for the leadership. I urged him not to, believing that would end in disaster.

In politics you do not do your opponent's work for them. If someone wants to bring on a challenge, you don't make it easy for them. Let them bring it and wear the odium that goes with it. There is also the downside that if you raise the leadership question, you may not like the answer you get. The question becomes an invitation. I had understood from our conversation that Malcolm had agreed with my advice.

I knew the week in Parliament would be challenging but expected we would get through it. As I left home in the Shire to drive to Canberra for Parliament, Jen asked me, "Will Malcolm be alright?" I said, "He'll be fine. All he has to do is sit tight and get through the week. On Thursday, Parliament will rise, colleagues will go back to their electorates, and things will settle down after that."

So the parliamentary week began like most others. Our leadership group met in the morning, and Monday passed without too much going on. On Tuesday, after our leadership meeting broke up, the PM asked his deputy leader, the foreign affairs minister, Julie Bishop, to stay behind. I thought nothing of it. While Julie met with Malcolm, the rest of us headed to the party room meeting.

The party room is where all of the members of Parliament from your own party, your side, gather on the first Tuesday of every fortnight when Parliament is in session to discuss party matters. The most important decision the party room ever makes is the election of the party leader. At any meeting, the leader can be challenged. This is what Malcolm had been talking about a few days before when he canvassed whether he should try to flush out any challengers by bringing on what is called a "leadership spill" himself. That is where you voluntarily vacate the leadership and force any challengers to nominate against you.

At the party room meeting that morning, everything changed. It was clear I had been mistaken about Malcolm taking my advice not to spill the leadership, or perhaps he had changed his mind and chosen not to tell me. That's okay; he was the PM, and that was his prerogative. The PM got up, declared the leadership vacant, and called on a ballot for leader. It was on.

I was shocked. I looked at Malcolm with an expression of surprise that asked, "What on earth are you doing?" He gazed back with that look of self-assurance and determination that I was used to. He was convinced that he had outsmarted them all.

The PM won the ballot 48 to 35, but, as I had feared, that margin would not be enough to stop what was coming. Instead, it precipitated the change Malcolm had been trying to avoid. The challengers had done better than they thought they would, and so they believed that, given a few more days, they could finish off the PM. So they set about piling on the pressure.

The seal had been broken. It would now be very difficult to stop the chain of events that would follow. Nevertheless, a number of us tried. Over the course of that week, I stood by the PM together with Julie; the defense industry minister, Christopher Pyne; and a few others. Late on Wednesday evening, as events were moving away from us, Malcolm told me in his office that I should begin thinking about running if he wasn't able to hang on.

While I was ambitious and had hoped one day to reach the top spot, it was not my preferred time to become PM. I supported the PM and thoroughly enjoyed my job as treasurer. Abbey and Lily were still very young, and I knew just how tough the job of PM was and what it would mean for our family. At that time I also believed Malcolm could win the next election, and I'd said so. As I considered what to do next, I had one rule: I would not be in any ballot against the current PM. I was not a challenger. If Malcolm was in the contest, then I was not. I resisted those who were urging me to run for the leadership and asked them to support Malcolm. I kept my peace.

In order to have a second meeting of the party room, a majority of members would have to sign a petition calling for a further meeting. This had the effect of slowing things down. For the challengers, requiring a petition was a big problem. It's one thing to get people to vote for you against the leader in a secret ballot. It is another to put pen to paper and publicly drag down your prime minister. It also meant that they had to maintain their momentum to keep the pressure on. The onus was now on them to produce the numbers to get the second meeting.

On the Thursday after Parliament had concluded (or "risen"), I suggested to the PM that since the requisite number of signatures had not been collected and Parliament had risen for the week, we should all just leave Canberra, as we usually did when Parliament had concluded, and allow things to calm down. We could then regroup in a couple of weeks' time, when we returned. I was still focused on getting the PM through the storm.

But Malcolm believed things had gone too far and would need to be resolved. He decided that if signatures of the majority of the party room came in, he would call the meeting. I assumed he would voluntarily vacate the leadership at this meeting, without the need for a ballot. At that point I said to the PM and others in the PM's office, "Well, I need to get busy," and left. At that time, I believed the campaign to save the PM was over. The question now was what I would do. The decision to step forward and contest the leadership of our governing party in such a tumultuous time could result in total humiliation and end my political career. Why would I risk all the hard work and sacrifice when success seemed so remote? Why not just sit this one out and wait for a better opportunity?

So often we are faced with encounters in life where we must confront the real measure of our faith. They can be painful and stressful, but they always help us to grow in our faith. We have to make decisions as we ask the hard questions about our faith. Do we really trust God? What are we prepared to do about it? For me this was another one of those times.

I had been praying about the situation all week. I had been seeking the counsel and fellowship of Christian friends and mentors. I was talking to Jen. I was reading God's Word. I weighed the practical possibilities, and I had a pretty good sense of the numbers we could count on. I sought the peace of God that surpasses all understanding, and He provided it (Philippians 4:7). At each stage I sought to be sensitive to the promptings of the Holy Spirit. All of this was necessary and helpful, but at the end of the day I still had to make the final decision of faith through obedience. I had to decide whether to step up or step off. After careful consideration, I decided that the path of obedience was to step up. So I raised my staff and walked toward the sea.

I hit the phones with my close colleagues and supporters. Lists of phone numbers of my parliamentary colleagues who would be voting in the ballot were brought to me. I worked my way steadily through each of the calls. Other than to sleep, I did not stop until minutes before the meeting to hold the ballot. The only people you can ever truly believe when you are canvassing for votes in a leadership ballot are the ones who say they are not going to vote for you. One call is never enough—you have to verify every expression of support through many other calls and contacts, which was done by my close supporters. We ignored the media. They were talking up the chances of the other candidates and didn't see me coming. I had never been the favorite of the political media in Canberra. Anyway, this contest was not going to be decided in the media. It was going to be decided by the members of Parliament who would be sitting in the room and voting, and I had the opportunity to speak directly to them all in advance of the meeting.

The day of a leadership ballot tends to be theatrical, as if acting out some Shakespearean drama. I was hoping it would not be a tragedy. Before these ballots, each of the candidates usually walks to the party room flanked by their supporters. The media run a long-angle camera shot of them all striding down the corridor together. I call this walk to the party room "The Parade." I had never liked these staged parades and had never been part of one. I found them melodramatic and pretentious. We didn't need to put on a show. I walked to the party room on my own. I messaged my pastor friends. I knew that regardless of the outcome, it was God who would be walking in there with me, it was God who would sustain me, and it was God who would be walking out with me, whatever the result.

To my surprise, instead of immediately declaring the leadership vacant and proceeding directly to the ballot, Malcolm called a ballot for the leadership to be spilled. My supporters and I had not contemplated this would happen. We had not discussed it or what each of us would do.

I voted against the motion. My view was that Malcolm should remain PM. Not all my close supporters shared my view. They had their own experiences and views regarding Malcolm's leadership and made their own decisions in that moment. The ballot was car-ried 45 to 40, which meant Malcolm had lost. The leadership was now vacant.

There was then a call for candidates for the leadership to stand. I rose to my feet along with Julie and the home affairs minister, Peter Dutton. Peter had led the challenge against Malcolm over the course of that week. While we were not personally close, there was no enmity between Peter and me. Peter and his supporters were doing what they believed to be right for our party and the govern-ment. I disagreed with them. I had not brought this challenge on. I had actively resisted it. But now that it was on, I believed I was best placed to carry our government forward and had made my case to my colleagues.

In what is called an exhaustive ballot, the candidate with the lowest number of votes in each round drops out. Julie was elimi-nated in the first round. It then came down to Peter and me. The final ballot was declared in my favor 45 to 40. I was now leader of the Liberal Party and would become Australia's thirtieth prime minister later that evening when sworn in by the governor general.

You always wonder how you will feel in such a moment. The first feeling is one of relief, followed by one of accomplishment. You can't allow yourself to enjoy it for too long, but you do allow yourself a brief moment. This quickly gives way to humility, overwhelming responsibility, and urgency. I rose to speak to my col-leagues. In my speech I acknowledged and thanked Malcolm for his service to our party and our country. I thanked Julie for the same. I congratulated Josh Frydenberg, my new deputy leader and soon-to-be treasurer, and thanked my colleagues for putting their faith in us. I then turned my attention to the significant work ahead. "You have asked me to lead," I said. "I am now asking you to follow." The task ahead was daunting. Our party was trailing in polling for the upcoming national election, and things were about to get a lot worse. It would be a hard road back to get the voters to stick with us. In my first speech to my colleagues, I made reference to Moses's successor, Joshua, at the battle of Jericho. I said that though the walls were high, we could bring them down and win the national election. I had a plan, and if we united and stuck to the plan, we could turn this around and win. I admit that few, if any, believed me at the time, though many wanted to.

The media jokingly began referring to me as "the night watchman." It was not a compliment. For those who don't know anything about Australia's national game, cricket, I'll try to use baseball terms to explain. Test cricket matches are played over five days. The night watchman is the batter you send in late in the day when some of your best batters have gotten out and you don't want to risk another good batter before the end of the day's play. So you send in one of your weaker batters. The night watchman is strictly told, "Don't be a hero; just make sure you don't get out before the end of the day's play." Hopefully, conditions will improve the next day, and after the night watchman inevitably gets out, your team can regroup and go on to make a good score. But no one expects the night watchman to hang around for long. We would still need a miracle.

More than once over the next eight months, I believed it was all hopeless. In late 2018, I was returning from a meeting of the G20 Leaders' Summit in Buenos Aires, attended by the presidents and prime ministers of the world's twenty largest economies. This followed soon after my first APEC Leaders' Meeting in Port Moresby in Papua New Guinea. I hadn't been looking forward to either of these events as there was just too much going on domestically in Australia. The summits would involve back-to-back meetings with world leaders who would be very mindful of the domestic political situation in Australia. While I expected they would be polite, I did not reasonably expect any of them to invest any real time in forming a relationship with me. I'm quite sure they would all have been told by their advisers that they would be unlikely to see this new guy from Australia again. This did not offend or surprise me. It was politics, not personal.

One leader who bucked this trend was US Vice President Mike Pence, whom I met in Port Moresby. Earlier in the day we had our formal bilateral meeting where we discussed the various issues in the Australia-US relationship. When we had completed our formal talks, I asked for a one-on-one discussion and for our aides to leave, which Mike readily agreed to. I was aware of Mike's faith and asked for us to pray together over the things we had discussed, which included the increasing assertiveness of China in our region. Later that evening we were seated together at dinner and we exchanged further stories of our faith. Mike offered me great encouragement, and we became friends. I formed a similarly strong Christian friendship with US Secretary of State Mike Pompeo and Papua New Guinea Prime Minister James Marape. I will always be thankful for God putting these friendships in my life.

On the long trip back from Buenos Aires across the Pacific, I was sitting in the PM's private cabin of our old Boeing Business Jet. I often found the private cabin in the PM's plane a bit of a refuge where I could do some thinking, get through my briefs, and catch up on some reading. My staff was always very respectful of my quiet time in the cabin. On this occasion, thirty thousand feet above the Pacific Ocean, I was dealing with yet another political crisis that threatened to end my administration.

As I sent a flurry of text messages into the Pacific night, there was also time to sit back and reflect on everything that was going on. I sent a message to my pastors' chat group asking them to pray for me. I wrote, "The world's voices are saying any chance of winning is over; they've written me off." I even said, "To be fair, under these circumstances they're not being unreasonable."

Reflecting on the many promises God had kept throughout my life, I finished off my message to the chat group, saying, "All I know is that I'm called to be faithful and obedient no matter what. Pray that I will live each day simply seeking to serve Him and trust." This was the breakthrough I needed. It did not result in the resolution of my immediate problems. Many of them continued, and not to my advantage. It did, however, strengthen me as I learned to put my trust in God and keep my eyes focused on Him as my "audience of one," no matter what. I believed this was the way for me to be the best prime minister I could possibly be for the people of Australia.

At the start of the following year I wrote again to my pastor friends: "Have been reflecting this morning that Joseph, Joshua, Gideon, and David were all just ordinary men like me. Passionate and able—yes—but no doubt vain, stubborn, imperfect, and given to fear. No doubt Joseph believed he would rot in prison. Joshua and Gideon would have been very alive to the likelihood of being killed in battle. David would have feared for his life as he fled from Saul.

"Part of my faith journey in this is being prepared to accept the consequences of standing for God. Humiliation and defeat may await me. If that is the price of standing for God in this world, then I must embrace it. The victory is always God's. The decision for me is the obedience of faith. I have been angry at God that things are not going better. It's not about that, it's about faith and obedience—not trusting in an earthly outcome, but just trusting. There are sixteen weeks to go [to the election]. It will feel like walking through the flames, but we have entered the furnace, and we are not alone, and we will emerge on the other side just as loved by God as when all this began."

Every time I have had to look into the abyss of uncertainty, there has only ever been one force that has consistently penetrated the void: the love of Jesus. This is why understanding God's blessing in our lives is so important. God has been writing His own story of blessing in my life and yours since before we were born (Psalm 139:14; Jeremiah 1:5; Galatians 1:15). Satan knows this and spends our lifetimes trying to convince us of the opposite—that we are unloved, forsaken, and alone. He seeks to take our eyes off God's many blessings in our lives and to hide them behind our trials, disappointments, and challenges.

Sixteen weeks later, I stood up with Jen, Abbey, and Lily in front of a cheering crowd at the Wentworth Hotel in Sydney after we had won on election night. I proclaimed, "I have always believed in miracles." It was my way of acknowledging God and seeking to give Him the glory.

A week before voters went to the polls, one of my close parliamentary colleagues asked me what Christians should pray for to be written on the front pages of the national newspapers the day after the election. I replied, without even thinking, "ScoMo's Miracle." In my office today I have a framed picture of the front page from one of Australia's major city newspapers published the day after the election with that exact headline.[1]

REAL FAITH

God is faithful, but believing events will turn out in your favor just because you are a Christian is neither true nor the point. That's not what faith is all about. I've won and lost elections as prime minister, but God is the same.

Real faith is about a life of obedience. It's about taking action in the circumstances we find ourselves in and trusting God with what comes next. Real faith is knowing that whether things turn out badly or well, our joy and security in life will be found in our obedience to His purposes and plans for our good, not our own or what the world considers success or failure. What are you going to do next? Do you have your staff (or cap) in hand? Are you ready to raise your staff and start walking toward the water of what God is calling you to?

Chapter Three

WHO DO YOU BELIEVE YOU ARE?

> *Peter turned around and saw the disciple whom*
> *Jesus loved following them—the one who also*
> *had leaned back on His chest at the supper.*
> JOHN 21:20

We left Blair House in Washington on a beautiful fall morning in 2019. We drove through the gates of the White House in a large, black, armor-plated Secret Service SUV on our way to the South Lawn. Waiting to greet us there was the president of the United States and the First Lady, a ceremonial guard, and hundreds of guests waving Australian and US flags.

Later that evening we would be the guests of honor at a Camelot-style state reception in the Rose Garden. It was quite incredible, right down to the combined military bands playing "Waltzing Matilda" on the rooftop of the White House overlooking the garden. It was like that scene in *Love Actually*, when the band pops up in the church at the end of the wedding and plays "All You Need Is Love."

That morning, as we drove through the gates of the White House for the first time, I reached over, took Jen's hand, and said to her, "Well, love, we're a long way from home."

I first met Jen when I was just eleven years old. It was a Saturday night at Luna Park, a popular amusement park next to the famous Sydney Harbour Bridge in North Sydney. Jen admitted many years later that she had liked me even then but thought I was a bit over-confident (some things never change). So she thought she'd just play it cool, keep an eye on me, and see what happened. There was no rush; she was only twelve.

We spent years in the same churches, going on fellowship out-ings and attending the regular round of Christian youth camps. It wasn't until an Easter camp in our final year of high school, sitting together on a Saturday night on the end of the jetty at Kiwi Ranch at Lake Munmorah, just north of Sydney, that we first held hands and started dating. I told the camp leader the next morning that Jen was the girl I wanted to marry. I was just sixteen.

Almost five years later, after we had both finished university, we got married at a little chapel in Oatley in southern Sydney. It was the best decision I have ever made, other than to follow Jesus. We had intended to travel to North America, where I was going to study divinity at Regent College in Vancouver, but life took us on a different path. I got offered a good job in Sydney. Dad told me I now had responsibilities as a married man and had a duty to settle down and take the job (which he had engineered, by the way—my father was pretty cunning). I followed my father's advice and took the job, which began my ultimate pathway into politics. I have always wondered where that other path may have taken us. Perhaps the same place?

It's not easy to be a politician's wife. Politics is a demanding and selfish business that robs the time, priority, attention, and appreciation that those you love have every right to expect from you. And it can leave you all feeling isolated, frustrated, alone, and empty. It is no wonder that so many politicians' marriages and families fail.

Jen has a reservoir of love that defies the natural. Thankfully, I haven't found the bottom yet. I have no doubt that I have come close on occasion. But Jen's love draws on something far more compelling than me. We both share a strong faith in Jesus Christ. This enables us to share in the security of God's love, which is the strongest foundation for any marriage, a threefold cord between us and God (Ecclesiastes 4:12). We would never hold ourselves out to be a perfect example to other couples. We are just thankful God has given us the grace, mercy, strength, and, above all, the love to make our life together work. I pray He will continue to do so.

YOU ARE WHAT YOU LOVE

Saint Augustine is believed to have said, "You are what you love." Jesus said it another way: "Where your treasure is, there your heart will be also" (Matthew 6:21). It's true. Who and what we love defines us. The love of power, the love of success, the love of honor and status, the love of pleasure, wealth, and comfort will all write a story about our life. We may not like how that story ends. A life driven by love for others creates an entirely different story.

To love others is to reflect the image of God in us. Human love is a conscious act of will. It is also the source of our human dignity. Love enlivens us and enables us to see the value and worth in others and to promote their worth above our own. This is next-level.

I believe this is precisely what God intended. We were made to love because we were made in God's image, and God is love (Genesis 1:27; 1 John 4:8).

First Corinthians 13:4–7 says, "Love is patient, love is kind. It does not envy, it does not boast, it is not proud. It does not dishonor others, it is not self-seeking, it is not easily angered, it keeps no record of wrongs. . . . It always protects, always trusts, always hopes, always perseveres" (NIV).

We were made to be in relationship with others, putting this love to work—loving your wife, your husband, your children, your parents, your extended family, your community, and the strangers who come into your life. All of this creates an entirely different you.

Despite extolling the virtues of love, the world still tries to define us by the superficial things of life that we strive to possess— our achievements, our job, our education, our families, our wealth, our appearance, or others' good opinions of us. Or it tries to define us negatively by our lack of those same things. In the age of identity politics, we are increasingly being defined by our gender, race, ethnicity, or sexuality. We can also allow ourselves to be defined by our pasts, our backgrounds, and the things we have done. Grounding our identity in the wrong foundations will shortchange us from the blessings of God and will blind us to the many blessings we already possess in Him.

In the Sermon on the Mount, Jesus told the story of the wise builder who builds his house on the rock and the fool who builds his house on the sand (Matthew 7:24–27). There is no shortage of beachfront real estate the world wants to sell us on the promise of how it will secure our identity. Yet the only real estate we should be interested in when it comes to really knowing who we are is found on the rock of the kingdom of God.

A LESSON IN FAILURE

We do it all the time. We meet someone new and the question inevitably gets asked: "So, what do you do?" The question is innocent enough, but it's actually a cultural proxy for "Who are you?" You may say you're a teacher or a nurse, or perhaps a prime minister. You may say you're raising your family or caring for aging parents. All are honest and decent occupations. But none of them speak to who you really are and your worth or dignity as a human being. In truly loving relationships we know that we are not loved because of what we do but because of who we are.

Jen doesn't love me because I was the prime minister and took her to meet the Queen at Buckingham Palace (although that was pretty cool). She knew me long before then. Jen loves me for who I am and looks at me through her lens of love. As a result, she looks for the best and can often see what I don't see (or what I lose sight of). And my love for Jen works the same way. God has an even better idea of who we really are, and He loves us more than any human being can—even our husbands, wives, parents, families, and friends.

As Christians we may think we don't define ourselves by what we do. But sometimes we don't appreciate what we really value until it's taken away. Have you ever lost a job? I have, and not just when I lost the election. The first time this happened to me I was in my late thirties. It was deeply humiliating and soul destroying.

I had enjoyed a successful career up until that point. I was the managing director of Australia's national tourism promotional agency, Tourism Australia. I led a team of about 150 people around the world with a budget of around $130 million a year with offices in places like LA, London, Shanghai, Tokyo, and Singapore while headquartered in Sydney.

The agency was owned and funded by the Australian government and overseen by an independent board of directors appointed by the minister for tourism. It was a great job. The changes I made at Tourism Australia generated both excitement and controversy. The increasing media profile that came my way from doing the job was not appreciated by my minister. I didn't handle that relationship well, and it deteriorated until the minister ultimately asked the prime minister, John Howard, to have me removed.

I had enjoyed a good relationship with Prime Minister Howard. I used to be one of his senior campaign managers. In two successive elections we had achieved record results in his home state of New South Wales, where I had been the campaign manager. John had been very supportive of my appointment at Tourism Australia and the work we were doing. He would later become an important mentor to me when I was PM. But on this occasion the politics demanded that I go. Moving me on was good politics, enabling the PM to lock in my minister's support for him. It wasn't personal; it was just politics.

In my mind I had it all mapped out. I had planned to continue in that high-profile role until an opportunity presented itself for me to run for Parliament. A Christian mentor of mine in politics, Bruce Baird, was considering retiring in a few years, which meant an opportunity might open up in his electoral district, where I could run for preselection (similar to a primary in the United States). But there was no hurry; I had a great job to see me through until that time came. Then, what felt like overnight, it all came tumbling down, and very publicly too. Not only had I blown it, but I had no idea what to do next. I was shell-shocked.

In the aftermath I was trying to figure out next steps and feeling sorry for myself when I had coffee with my pastor at the time, Joel A'Bell. He hit me between the eyes with a powerful word. "Mate," he said, "you need to understand that you aren't what you do. You need to start seeing yourself as God does. He doesn't care what your job is, He just loves you."

As much as I hated to admit it, I had built up this image of myself in my own mind as a successful person who was going places. I had worked hard, pouring my efforts into my work, telling myself I was doing this out of a profound sense of purpose and a desire to set up a good future for myself and Jen. I'd also let myself believe I had been the architect of my success. I had vested far too much of my own sense of identity in my purpose, vocation, and status. This was sandy ground. I had bought the full beachfront block. The newly built house looked great. But when the storm hit, it crumbled. I felt worthless.

Joel helped me understand that God was much more interested in His relationship with me than in what I did. We don't have to prove anything to God, even the things we think we are doing for Him. God's love has nothing to do with what we think we can offer. He loves us just as we are, in all our brokenness. God's love is transformational if you allow it to be. It's one thing to accept it; it's entirely another to let it transform you and allow you to see yourself through His eyes instead of through the perspective of what you have or haven't accomplished.

Jen and I moved to the Shire in southern Sydney. Bruce announced his intention to retire, and I sought preselection for the next federal election. The outcome would be far from certain. I put everything on hold to run a solid preselection campaign. I declined some job offers along the way and made ends meet by starting a small consulting business. We had

God's love has nothing to do with what we think we can offer.

also just been blessed with the birth of our first daughter, Abbey. Then I lost. I didn't even come close. I was basically jobless again, my career was stalled, and I had a new daughter to take care of. Strangely, this time the failure was not accompanied by the awful feeling of shame and loss that had surrounded me when I lost my job at Tourism Australia, even though the consequences were arguably far worse.

This time there was peace flowing from a deeper relationship with God. I was secure in Him. I had invested in my relationship with Him. I had been studying God's promise in Deuteronomy 31:8: "He will not desert you or abandon you. Do not fear and do not be dismayed." I had put my trust in Him. I had reflected deeply on the many blessings of God in my life and was truly thankful, especially for the recent gift of our daughter. What I knew from the security of my relationship with God was that whatever happened, God was not going to leave me, Jenny, and Abbey stranded. Some months later, the preselection was remarkably overturned, and I was preselected as the party's new candidate. I ran in the next election and entered the Australian Parliament later that year as the federal member for Cook.

Never again would my success or failure determine my identity or worth. Nor did I fool myself that the opportunities I had to serve were a function of my own cleverness or design. I accepted those opportunities as gifts from God to serve for the season for which they were intended. When I lost the prime ministership at the general election in 2022, it was the second time I had lost a big job. And it was very, very public. But I knew I had served faithfully and to the best of my ability. I knew that my season of service in government had ended. I knew that I had been loved by Jesus before I served, that I had been loved by Jesus during my term, and that His love would continue long after my term had ended. I would now return to our life in the Shire. It would also be a time to rejuvenate as we waited for whatever God had in store for us next.

It is often the case that when politicians lose high office they acquire what we call "relevance deprivation syndrome." Since losing the election, I have not suffered from this affliction, because I learned my identity has nothing to do with the power and authority that came with being prime minister. That was just my job—one I loved doing and considered a great privilege. Instead, my identity was grounded in my relationship with God and His love for me. In fact, despite the natural disappointment of the loss and my great regret for the impact it had on my colleagues and my country, I was now happily experiencing "irrelevance appreciation syndrome."

FEARFULLY AND WONDERFULLY MADE

Not long after I joined Parliament I became involved in a small group of parliamentarians who gathered to discuss passages from the Bible, talk about our lives and the challenges we faced, and pray for one another. It soon ended up meeting in my office. This continued while I was prime minister. I just loved the idea that every week when Parliament was sitting, even if I couldn't be there, my fellow members of parliament (MPs) would be sitting in my office suite praying for one another and for our country.

At the start of my prime ministership, one of the members of our group, a Jewish colleague named Julian Leeser, introduced me to the writings of the now late Rabbi Lord Jonathan Sacks.

Sacks's teaching focused heavily on how human beings are made in God's image (Genesis 1:26) and therefore possess a dignity that is specific and inalienable,[1] underlying our belief that we are free and responsible, not merely the victims of necessity and chance.[2] Sacks argued that appreciating the inherent dignity of all human beings is the foundation for the morality needed to sustain a functional society.[3]

Sacks taught that if we depart from or reject fundamental beliefs about our unique worth as created human beings, we enter very dangerous territory, both personally and as a society. But when we appreciate our own unique human dignity of being fearfully and wonderfully made, as described in Psalm 139:14, we are better able not only to appreciate our own worth but also to honor the image of God in other people.

It is true that Jesus was unambiguous when He said, "From the beginning of creation, God created them male and female" (Mark 10:6). But it is also important to appreciate that our creation was not limited to our physical being. In Psalm 139, David talked about the creation of his "innermost parts," his "formless substance," his "days that were ordained," and the precious and countless thoughts God had for David in his creation (vv. 13–18).

There is a reason the Bible starts by describing our beginnings. It says in Genesis 1:1, "In the beginning God created the heavens and the earth." The Gospel of John in the New Testament starts in the same way: "In the beginning was the Word, and the Word was with God, and the Word was God. He was in the beginning with God. *All things came into being through Him, and apart from Him not even one thing came into being that has come into being*" (1:1–3, emphasis added). He wanted us to know right from the start where we came from, who put us here, and why this is important to living a full life.

We deny and ignore the truth and significance of our creation, and creation more broadly, at our peril. Also at our own peril, we pretend we are equal to our Creator, or we elevate any created thing by idolizing it and thus making it equal in our eyes to our Creator.

John went on to write, "In Him was life, and the life was the

Light of mankind" (1:4). We are given this life from our Creator. It is not an accident; it is purposeful and intentional. You are not a mistake or accident, and neither is anyone else. God is deliberate (Proverbs 16:4). He has plans for your good because He created you. Your life is unique, sacred, and precious. Your life is not something to be treated casually by you or anyone else, nor is anyone else's life.

During the pandemic I was asked by the media one day, before the vaccine had been developed, why I was taking actions to combat the virus that were inconvenient to many younger people, who were more resistant to the severe impacts of COVID-19, in order to protect the lives of vulnerable older citizens, who were basically just going to die anyway. I was horrified by the logic. My response was immediate: "Because as prime minister I see every Australian's life as precious."

If you see the dignity and worth of another person, the beating heart in front of you, in all of its complexity, you're less likely to disrespect them. You're less likely to show contempt or hatred for them or, in today's fashion, seek to cancel them. Furthermore, awareness of our own failings and vulnerabilities enables us to be more accepting and understanding of the failings and vulnerabilities of others. We should respond with a humble heart, not a pious or judgmental one.

Respecting human dignity is at odds with the growing tendency to commodify fearfully and wonderfully made human beings by turning them into a banal set of physical and cultural attributes through modern-day identity politics: gender, race, ethnicity, language, age, sexuality, and so on. It diminishes our humanity.

When we reduce ourselves to such attributes, we limit ourselves and our agency. We descend into a tribalism that sees our identity through the prism of shared attributes and collective grievance. We lose sight of and forfeit who we actually are as individual human beings, in all our rich complexity, in all our wholeness and wonder, as we were created.

Throughout history we've seen what happens when people are defined solely by the group they belong to or an attribute they may have. The Jewish community may understand this better than any other in the world, but sadly it has not been the only one. Identity politics must be actively resisted, especially by Christians, in the name of human dignity. We are all fearfully and wonderfully made.

A NEW CREATION

In early January 2021 I was returning to Canberra after spending a short summer break at the beach with my family and our close friends on the south coast of New South Wales. I had just left Jen and the girls behind since they were staying for a little longer, so I was feeling a bit sad and lonely. On the three-hour drive back to Canberra I listened to a sermon by Pastor Rick Warren, author of the bestselling book *The Purpose Driven Life*.[4]

Pastor Rick was reflecting on the extraordinary events of the past year, which had included the US presidential election and the assault on Congress. In his sermon Pastor Rick encouraged Christians to dedicate themselves to their relationship with God as we entered another year of uncertainty. In particular he encouraged us to really commit to a daily discipline of reading God's Word. I was inspired by Pastor Rick's sermon and took up the challenge.

As prime minister, the minute you open your eyes each morning you are bombarded with information. Your smartphone is bursting with the overnight intelligence reports, the morning media summaries, text messages from your colleagues and senior staff, further details and changes to your daily program, and any number of other issues demanding your immediate attention. You wake up with your phone screaming at you. Some mornings you dread waking up because you know what will be there to greet you.

Even if you're not the prime minister, it is very easy to fall into the habit of allowing what is beaming into your smartphone every morning to set the tone and mood for your day and let that get in your spirit. I saw Pastor Rick's challenge as an opportunity to try to break this cycle and do something different. While prayer and Bible reading had always been part of my routine, I tended to do it in the evening when things were quieter. In taking up Pastor Rick's challenge, I decided that every morning, before I would read the myriad reports, emails, and texts on my smartphone, I would now click on my Bible app and progressively read my way sequentially through the entire Bible, cover to cover. It took me around eighteen months.

Those eighteen months were the most difficult I have ever experienced, including the ultimate loss and aftermath of the 2022 general election. But working my way through the Bible each day enabled God to get in the first word every morning, before the torrent started. I kept notes along the way. In many ways those notes were the inspiration for the book you are now reading.

When I was reading the history of the kings of Israel and Judah in the books of Samuel, Kings, and Chronicles, I was struck by the story of Hezekiah, who refused to let himself be defined by his family's past. Time after time we read that the kings of Israel and Judah did evil in the sight of the Lord and did not turn from the sins of their fathers and were buried with them. Over almost 450 years and forty-three rulers, there were just seven good kings.

One of the worst kings was Hezekiah's father, Ahaz, who ruled Judah for sixteen years. This guy would have made the producers of *Game of Thrones* blush. He even sacrificed his own children (2 Kings 16:3). When Hezekiah was born, you could be forgiven for thinking he did not stand a chance of surviving, let alone of becoming a good king, with a father like Ahaz. Based on all the earlier episodes, you could have just assumed Hezekiah would go the same way as his depraved father, like so many kings before and after him. But that's not what happened.

Hezekiah actually turned out to be a good king. Hezekiah put an end to the abominable practices of his father and sought to turn his nation back to God. He restored the temple, listened to the prophets like Isaiah, struck down the idols, and trusted God when his kingdom was attacked (2 Kings 18:4–5; 2 Kings 19). Not a bad effort.

Of course, Hezekiah also had his off days and made some pretty big mistakes as well. All leaders do (I know I did). Despite his mistakes, the Bible still says there was no king quite like him, before or after (2 Kings 18:5). What an extraordinary transformation in just one generation. Hezekiah refused to let his heritage or past define him.

We can often think we are prisoners of our past or that our future has already been written for us. This can be because of who our parents may have been, where we have come from, or what we have experienced, including suffering abuse by those we were supposed to be able to trust. It can also be a result of what we have done—our regrets, our failures, our sins.

We have all done things in our lives that we shouldn't have done and wish we hadn't. We all have sinned (Romans 3:23). These experiences can work to destroy our image of ourselves and our sense of worth. We then become prisoners of our past, thinking, *How could anyone now love me, knowing where I have come from, what's happened to me, or what I have done?* But this is a lie. Our bitter experiences, failures, and sins lie to us, telling us we are worthless. They judge and accuse us. They tell us our identity is so damaged that we can never live down our past or our heritage, let alone be forgiven.

This may be the case in this world, but in God's kingdom that's just not true. Hezekiah chose to live in God's kingdom, and it changed the course of his life and his nation. Scripture says, "Hezekiah put his whole trust in the GOD of Israel. . . . He held fast to GOD—never loosened his grip. . . . And GOD, for his part, held fast to him through all his adventures" (2 Kings 18:5–6 MSG). Hezekiah chose to be transformed through his relationship with God. His identity was not grounded in who his earthly father was or the experiences of his upbringing but in a restored relationship with God. We can choose the same.

> We do not have to allow our past failures, setbacks, and heritage to determine our identity.

We do not have to allow our past failures, setbacks, and heritage to determine our identity. God has brought about a better way, through relationship with Him, made possible by His love, which gives all of us a fresh start, whether we think we deserve it or not. As Paul told the Corinthians, "If anyone is in Christ, this person is a new creation; the old things passed away; behold, new things have come" (2 Corinthians 5:17). This means "there is now no condemnation at all for those who are in Christ Jesus" (Romans 8:1) and "your life is hidden with Christ in God" (Colossians 3:3).

ONE WHO JESUS LOVES

Another of Rabbi Sacks's teachings is that "to be a Jew is to be defined by the One who loves us."[5] This is actually true for all of us. And there is no one who loves us more than God. We are defined not only by who and what we love but by Who loves us. The apostle

John knew this. He would often describe himself in his own gospel as the disciple Jesus loved (John 13:23; 21:7).

I remember Pastor Joseph Prince from Singapore preaching in Sydney one night and explaining that this was not because John was the only disciple Jesus actually loved. Of course Jesus loved them all. But it was only John in Scripture who chose to see himself, to define himself, through that lens of God's love. This was how John chose to understand his own identity. If you asked John to tell you a bit about himself, he would have just said, "I'm the one who Jesus loved." He needed no more definition than that. He felt complete in the love of Jesus.

We see this throughout all of John's writings in the Bible. He constantly spoke of the love of God: "For God so loved the world, that He gave His only Son" (John 3:16); "Beloved, let's love one another; for love is from God, and everyone who loves has been born of God and knows God. The one who does not love does not know God, because God is love. By this the love of God was revealed in us, that God has sent His only Son into the world so that we may live through Him. In this is love, not that we loved God, but that He loved us" (1 John 4:7–10).

In Charles Wesley's great hymn "And Can It Be," he wrote in verse 3,

> *He left His Father's throne above,*
> *So free, so infinite His grace;*
> *Emptied Himself of all but love,*
> *And bled for Adam's helpless race;*
> *'Tis mercy all, immense and free;*
> *For, O my God, it found out me.*
> *Amazing love! how can it be,*
> *That Thou, my God, should die for me!*

God's love is the rock you can build your identity upon—not what you do, not your physical attributes or what groups you belong to, and not your past. God's love is the true source of who you are. It is where you will find the foundation for your true identity. It is also true that we are who we love; and as children of God, we are to live out that love in our homes, in our communities, and anywhere else we can, even loving our enemies. But even greater than that, we are loved by God, and that changes everything else. So when asked, "Who are you?" let's say with John that we are simply the one who Jesus loves. That's more than enough.

> *God's love is the true source of who you are. It is where you will find the foundation for your true identity.*

Part Two

HOW SHOULD
I LIVE?

Finding Your Pathway

*Walking out your faith and your relationship with God
on a day-to-day basis is the hard part. The good news is
that God has equipped us to do just that. When we keep to
His path, His blessings are much easier to see and access.*

Chapter Four

WHAT OFFENDS YOU?

"Blessed is any person who does not take offense at Me."
MATTHEW 11:6

January 26, 1788, was not a good day for William Roberts. William had arrived at Sydney Cove after a long and treacherous voyage from Portsmouth, bunkered down in the light-starved bowels of the convict ship the *Scarborough* with 207 other convicts.[1] The *Scarborough* was one of eleven ships that comprised the First Fleet, led by Captain Arthur Phillip, sent to establish a new prison colony in New South Wales following Britain's loss of the American colonies in the recent Revolutionary War.

William had grown up in the small village of St. Keverne in Cornwall. He had married and was raising a young family. This all came to a shuddering halt when he was arrested for stealing five and a half pounds of yarn valued at nine shillings. He was convicted and sentenced to be transported to New South Wales, on the other side of the world, for seven years. At that time they may just as well have said they were sending him to the moon. He would never see his family or homeland again.[2]

Reverend Johnson was the chaplain of the First Fleet and the new colony. He was an evangelical clergyman who had been recommended for the job by William Wilberforce, the great anti-slavery campaigner. Reverend Johnson preached his first sermon on February 3, 1788, under the gum trees at Sydney Cove.[3] William Roberts was likely in attendance (it was compulsory). Johnson's text was Psalm 116:12: "What should I render unto the Lord for His benefits towards me?"[4] While the congregation was probably grateful to have survived the perilous voyage, it would be a stretch to imagine they considered their new circumstances a blessing.

After returning to England, the *Scarborough* came back to New South Wales a few years later as part of the notorious Second Fleet. It was joined by the *Neptune*, which was transporting Kezia Brown, who was convicted of stealing clothes.[5] Seventy-eight female convicts, some with children and infants, were all accommodated on the *Neptune*, as were 420 male convicts. The contractors were paid for each convict who embarked on the voyage, but there was no financial incentive to ensure the convicts arrived alive. During Kezia's voyage, more than a quarter of the convicts died, more than a third arrived sick, and 124 died soon after arriving.[6]

Reverend Johnson reported the misery of the scene of their arrival. He said it was "indescribable . . . their heads, bodies, clothes, blankets, were all full of lice. They were wretched, naked, filthy, dirty, lousy, and many of them—utterly unable to stand, or even to stir hand or foot."[7]

Australia's colonial beginnings were marked by cruelty, deprivation, and starvation. It was far from certain the colony would even survive, leaving all who had been banished there as forsaken and stranded on the other side of the world, in a land they did not understand. As a brutal penal colony, Australia's modern beginnings were very different from the pilgrim settlements of New England, where the faithful fled to escape religious persecution. Australia's Christian history and culture is quite different from that of the United States. "One Nation under God" and "In God We Trust" have never been mottos in our cultural story in Australia (although many of us wish they were).

Awful cruelty, terrible suffering, and dispossession were also inflicted on our indigenous peoples who had been living on our continent for more than sixty thousand years, comprising more than five hundred separate nations and 250 languages.[8] Aboriginal Australians were decimated not just by disease and alcohol but also by mindless violence born of fear, ignorance, and the dehumanization of indigenous peoples that was typical of the time.

This was not unique to Australia. Following the Renaissance, the life and culture of indigenous peoples were devastated throughout the world as expanding European empires scoured the globe laying claim to "new world" territories.

A few years after their arrival, William and Kezia were married in Sydney. After finishing their sentences, they moved to the Hawkesbury region, west of Sydney town, and became farmers, carving out a future for themselves and their family in a harsh colonial environment.[9] They were like so many others whose sacrifice and determination to survive would build a new nation, of which I am extremely proud.

Two hundred and thirty years after William arrived at Sydney Cove, his fifth great-grandson became Australia's thirtieth prime minister. January 26 is Australia's national holiday. In my first Australia Day address as prime minister, I paid tribute to my fifth great-grandparents, William and Kezia, and visited their graves with Jen and the girls to say thank you. The wonder of our country is that from such hardship and cruelty emerged a fair, decent, and prosperous nation that has positively impacted our world. Australia has become a standard bearer for freedom, prosperity, and democracy. We are also a country reconciling with our past and the treatment of our indigenous peoples.

When Australia was established as a federated nation in 1901, the topic of Reverend Johnson's first sermon returned in the opening text of our Constitution: "Whereas the people . . . , humbly relying on the blessing of Almighty God, have agreed to unite in one indissoluble Federal Commonwealth."[10]

In the new century, Christianity was the dominant mainstream influence on Australian cultural life, peaking during the postwar boom of the 1950s and 1960s. It was also during this time that we saw many new migrants come to Australia from postwar Europe, bringing with them their own religious lives and cultures. This would be followed by further waves of migrants from Asia and the Middle East in the 1970s and 1980s.

In 1961 almost 90 percent of Australians nominally identified themselves as Christian.[11] By 2001, this proportion had fallen to 68 percent.[12] At the same time, those identifying as having no religion had doubled to over 15 percent since 1971.[13]

In the most recent 2021 census, a watershed was reached. Almost two in five Australians now identified as having no religion, less than half (44 percent) identified as Christian, while a further 10 percent identified with other religions.[14] Australia is no longer a nominally Christian nation.

This trend also holds true beyond Australia. Over the past three generations, Western society has become untethered from its Christian origins. In the United Kingdom and New Zealand, Christians are also nominally in the minority.[15] Canada will soon follow.[16] In the United States around 70 percent of Americans still claim a Christian affiliation, but this number is declining.[17] That said, Christianity continues to forge ahead in the developing world. Secularism may have made significant inroads in the West, but Christianity remains the world's dominant religion.

The common question for Christians in Western nations, then, is, What is God up to in the midst of these changes? If His plans are always for good, and if God is apparently directing history toward His ultimate purposes for it, where does the turn away from Christianity and even the growing hostility toward faith in Jesus play into that?

I believe there are things going on in Western society that we, as a church, can learn from to make ourselves a more faithful bride to our Bridegroom, Jesus. Individually, too, we face a call to choose whether we will hold fast to Jesus, take an easier route, or just give up and complain about how our society is going to seed while we wait for Christ's return. The time in which we live is not an easy time to be a Christian, and the near future may become even harder, but God is neither surprised nor stymied by what we see. The Light of the World has a way of shining through, no matter what. As Christians, we are supposed to let Him shine through us.

OUR OWN GODS

In the Australia I grew up in, kids went to Sunday School or had their first Holy Communion at the local Catholic church. There was a prevailing assumption about the acceptance of Christian truths and that we were, culturally at least, a Christian society. The Reverend Billy Graham packed the Randwick Racecourse in Sydney in the late 1970s. My father took me and my brother, Alan, every night. Things are very different now. Deep cultural secularism is now taking the place of Christianity. You could say it is taking a stronghold. Perhaps all that has changed is the removal of the cultural veneer of Christianity in our society.

When I lost the prime ministership in the 2022 election, Australians elected probably the most deeply secular Parliament in our history. While those who profess a Christian faith may lament this outcome, it does reflect modern Australian society. In a democracy, our politics, our laws, our institutions, our schools, our public health systems, and our foreign policies all reflect what is going on in the hearts and minds of our people. The will of the majority prevails. Christians, Christian thinking, and Christian morality are increasingly in the minority. Generations are now growing up across the Western world without any knowledge of, interest in, or contact with Christianity, let alone evangelical Christianity.

Given that the Judeo-Christian tradition is the philosophical foundation of Western civilization and the liberty and democracy we enjoy, the implications of such a shift could be profound. Once our society is untethered from these moral, philosophical, and sociocultural moorings, where will we drift? We're about to find out.

Rod Dreher, author of *The Benedict Option*, notes that in 1798 John Adams wrote, "Our Constitution was made only for a moral and religious people. It is wholly inadequate to the government of any other."[18] Dreher concludes that "Adams understood that liberty under the Constitution could only work if the people were virtuous."[19] Dreher then went further, quoting de Tocqueville's *Democracy in America*: "Democracies will succeed only if 'mediating institutions,' including the churches, thrive."[20] This is the problem of libertarianism in a moral vacuum. There are no divine and objective restraints on our worst appetites or selves. In this scenario, our destruction can likely become the most extreme expression of our individual liberty.

It would be a mistake to think these changes mean there has been a change in the appetite for religious belief. Quite the contrary, actually. Western society has not become more atheist, and as I noted earlier, the world as a whole is not becoming less religious. In secular society, people still believe in god; they just believe god is looking back at them in the mirror. We believe ourselves to be our own gods. This dangerously unhinges society from any objective truth or morality beyond ourselves. If we are our own god, then we can define our own truth. We can just make up what suits us. Moral relativism rises to the top. As a result, the rules of morality and society in the Western world are being rewritten. The West is now doing what Paul referred to in Romans 1:25 as exchanging "the truth of God for falsehood." "Woe to those who are wise in their own eyes and clever in their own sight!" (Isaiah 5:21) seems like a timely warning for this new secular age.

The passion we see for many political causes on the left and right speaks to an energized secular morality where political activism is replacing traditional religion as the source of meaning and purpose. Climate action, social justice, gender and race politics, cancel culture, and the denunciation of capitalism are now fueling the passions and moral purpose of younger citizens in Western democracies. Such religious fervor is not confined to the political left.

One thing I have noticed about the adherents to all these new secular political faiths is that morality is conveniently externalized. They are focused on the sins of others rather than dealing with their own. True Christianity could not be more different from this worldview. Earnest political convictions do not compensate for one's own struggle with morality. Motives don't justify means any more than means justify ends.

In the same way, the focus on projection orients the belief system away from engaging human relationships and reconciliation and toward tyranny. In this worldview, others are a problem to be removed or canceled rather than people to engage with, live with, and love. The opportunity for peace, respect, tolerance, understanding, and humility, born of an appreciation of shared human frailty and common creation in God's image, is surrendered to self-righteousness. This practice of excommunication is exacerbated by the all-or-nothing hyper partisanship that now accompanies modern-day politics. In such a binary conception, the possibility that complex human beings can possess both positive and negative moral qualities is seen as impossible. This is absurd and juvenile.

In this worldview, those who don't agree with you are the problem. Worse, they are actually "bad people" not capable of doing what is right (as you see it). They are wrongly motivated and therefore can't be trusted to do good. Even if they do manage to do something positive, there is no way it was motivated by the same good motives you hold, so they can still be dismissed. They remain the problem. In this paradigm, it is up to the "good people" to set things right. Only the good people can do this. They have the right motives. They see things the right way. There are no prizes for guessing who the good people are; it's those who agree with you. Christians are not immune to this thinking.

When people see the world this way, anything is possible, and not in a good way. This justifies any action citizens take because they believe that their cause is pure and they are in the right. In the extreme, the same justification is used by fanatics to justify terrorism and was used by Christian rulers in the Middle Ages to justify the Crusades. Rabbi Sacks warned that when this thinking takes hold, the first casualty is always respect for human dignity.[21]

People are dehumanized for the sake of a righteous cause and become collateral damage. From that point it is not a long march to the Reign of Terror during the French Revolution, the Turkish genocide of Armenians, Hitler's genocide of the Jews, Mao's Cultural Revolution, Stalin's death camps, Pol Pot's killing fields, and the Rwandan genocide. This is what happens when such views are institutionalized and industrialized. It's truly terrifying. We need to wake up to the danger of this thinking. We have seen it all before—and ignored it all before—to humanity's great peril. Human beings are far more complex. There is good and bad in us all; none of us is perfect. In the *Gulag Archipelago*, Aleksandr Solzhenitsyn observed that "the line separating good and evil passes not through states, nor between classes, nor between political parties either—but right through every human heart—and through all human hearts."[22] Coming to terms with this dichotomy and reality is one of the great lessons of our Christian faith and life. We contend with the good and bad in each of us; that is where the real battle is. It is within, not without.

Christian faith is about the dramatic intervention of God in our lives to transform us and liberate us from "the body of this death" that Paul spoke of in Romans 7:24. This is not achieved by our striving toward God but the reverse. It is about recognizing God's agency in our own lives, at His initiation, and humbly accepting our helplessness. Christianity is the only religion in the world that is based on God reaching out to us rather than us believing we are able to satisfy the requirements of a holy and eternal God.

If we are constantly focused on the sins of others, where is the time to encounter ourselves, our own morality, and the lessons this encounter holds for us? It is not for us to judge others. That is God's job, not mine. Where is the opportunity to learn from each other, to live with each other? Our task and even expectation in such a complex world is not necessarily to agree, but to disagree better. This is not something our Western political environment is doing very well, and it is getting worse. It is compounded by the acceleration of social media, the hyper partisanship of modern politics, and how this has infected the Fourth Estate, where political activism, celebrity, and partisanship are being redefined as journalism, including in the mainstream media.

THE DIFFERENCE BETWEEN FAITH AND POLITICS

In Jordan Peterson's *12 Rules for Life: An Antidote to Chaos*, rule six says, "Set your house in perfect order before you criticize the world."[23] Peterson boldly calls out the problem of externalizing morality, charging, "Don't blame capitalism, the radical left, or the iniquity of your enemies. Don't reorganize the state until you have ordered your own experience. Have some humility. If you cannot bring peace to your household, how dare you try to rule a city?"[24] Peterson doesn't stop there. He says, "Aim high. Set your sights on the betterment of Being. Align yourself, in your soul, with Truth and the Highest Good. There is habitable order to establish and beauty to bring into existence. There is evil to overcome, suffering to ameliorate, and yourself to better."[25]

Peterson explains that all of this narrative comes from Jesus' Sermon on the Mount, which he describes as "the culmination ethic of the canon of the west."[26] Peterson regularly references the Bible in his writings, appreciating and respecting the Bible as an ancient wisdom text that distills significant moral and cultural learnings through its survival over the ages. Central to Peterson's writing is the need for individuals to take greater responsibility for their own lives.

None of this is to diminish the relevance of the issues that people are concerned about in politics. They are all important and must be contended with; however, such causes are not a replacement for the gospel of Jesus Christ. Whether it is advocating action on climate change or resisting the creeping menace of cultural Marxism in Western society, these are all valid subjects of politics. They should be debated and addressed through the democratic and political process, and I have views on all of them. I'll save those for another conversation. Christians should contest these issues in the political domain, as in any other. There are also strong scriptural bases for such political actions and stands. But let's be wary and wise not to fall into the trap of framing God into our own political agendas.

In Joshua 5:13 we read how, before the battle of Jericho, Joshua "raised his eyes and looked, and behold, a man was standing opposite him with his sword drawn in his hand." Given that Joshua was likely surveying the ground where the battle would be fought the next day, there was every possibility that he had been discovered by an enemy scout. So he asked the obvious question, "Are you for us or for our enemies?"

The answer was strange. The man said, "No." What did he mean? Was it "No, I am not with you" or "No, I am not with your enemy"? But the man with the big sword just said, "No." He then said, "I have come now as captain of the army of the LORD." The point here is that he had come to fight the Lord's battle, not Joshua's. Joshua was in God's army, not the other way around. Our duty is to align with God, not to conscript Him to our own causes and ambitions, no matter how worthy or sanctified we feel they are. This is the danger we must be wary of when we engage in the political arena as Christians.

Many Jews at the time of Jesus, especially the Sadducees,

> *Our duty is to align with God, not to conscript Him to our own causes and ambitions, no matter how worthy or sanctified we feel they are.*

believed the Messiah would rid them of the Romans. But Jesus actually said the opposite. Jesus understood there would always be "Romans" for people of faith to contend with in this world and that these opponents would come and go with the times. Jesus said, "Render to Caesar what is Caesar's but be born again yourself" (Matthew 22:21). Jesus preached a personal message of His love conquering and transforming us individually, not the overthrow of worldly regimes. His battle was for His people; that is what He came to fight for. His victory in this battle, and the witness of all who followed Him, would end up changing the world, more than any political movement could ever do and ever has.

Politics is not religion. And your faith is not your politics. It is more important than that. So please don't cheapen it. Rabbi Sacks expressed a similar view, saying, "When religion becomes political or politics becomes religious, the result is disastrous to religion and politics alike."[27] Again, this is not to suggest that Christians should not be involved in politics or that our beliefs do not intersect, or even clash, with politics. Of course we are called into this vocation, just like any other. Of course we must stand for the truth of God. But Christians in politics must be careful and humble when it comes to God's agency and their own political objectives. It is God who does the anointing, not us. Let's make sure we are on God's side.

Most Christians will share many of the same motives when it comes to political issues: love, justice, compassion, kindness, and integrity, to name a few. However, not all Christians will share the same political views about how these things should be accomplished. Christians were often some of my most vocal and judgmental critics in politics. In making their political arguments against me, sometimes they would even go so far as to call into question my own faith. They would basically claim God was on their side, not mine.

I would simply respond that as a citizen they were welcome to judge my policies, as I was accountable to them as citizens, but only God could judge my faith. That was between me and God.

King Solomon reminded us that "many are the plans in a person's heart, but it is the LORD's purpose that prevails" (Proverbs 19:21 NIV). So let's commit to the Lord whatever we purpose to do, including in politics. Let's be humble in submitting our plans and trusting Him. I had a plan to win an election. If we truly submit our plans, we can be okay whatever the outcome because we know that God's plans are for our good. Failing to bring one of my plans to fruition is not God admonishing or rejecting me; it is just God sticking with *His* plans for my good. I'm good with that.

TAKING OFFENSE

As Western society increasingly rejects the Judeo-Christian God, we are seemingly becoming more fragile and precious—by which I mean we are easily offended and, worse still, afraid of being offended. This denies us one of the most important learning experiences of being human—the ability to contend with views other than our own.

This is fast becoming the age where the right not to be offended has been elevated above the right to free speech in a liberal society. Emotions take precedence over rationality, perhaps even over authority. It is one of the many new entitlements. The modern secular world prides itself on tolerance. Yet it would seem the one thing it is unwilling to tolerate is being offended.

As emotional beings, we are easily offended. "I am offended; therefore I am" could be the mantra of our modern age, an age of offense. You cannot look at your smartphone news feed without reading about someone, somewhere, being offended. Apparently this is "news." Social media has accelerated and amplified this trend.

We all get offended in our lives. We have undoubtedly offended others, including those we love. I know I have. Such offenses can be quite legitimate and involve insensitivity, injustice, tragedy, betrayal, and violation. At other times our ignorance, insecurity, vanity, selfishness, or prejudice can lead us to taking offense in a situation.

Still, when you're offended, it hurts. This is human. However, holding on to your offense is where the damage really gets done. We can hold on to and nurse our offense like a wounded puppy, tending to its every need. We replay it constantly in our minds as it grows greater and more significant in our consciousness. At best, it steals our joy in life. At worst, it can take over our lives. Our grievance can begin to define us and can even lead us to believe it gives our lives meaning and purpose.

The world pretends we can protect everyone from offense. This is foolishness and can also be harmful. God did not promise us a life free of offense. As we have discussed, Scripture says we will have trials and tribulations in this life and will suffer (1 Peter 4:19).

Social psychologist Jonathan Haidt and his coauthor Greg Lukianoff have argued that increasing sensitivity to offense in our Western culture has led to coddling the minds of young people and disabling them from building the resilience necessary to lead positive and successful lives. In *The Coddling of the American Mind*, Haidt and Lukianoff report their research into the student population in American universities.[28] They observe that protecting young people from every possible negative emotional experience is damaging their resilience and increasing their likelihood of becoming fragile, anxious, and easily hurt. Haidt and Lukianoff cite the following as an example:

Columbia University's "Core Curriculum" . . . features a course called Masterpieces of Western Literature and Philosophy . . . (including) works by Ovid, Homer, Dante, Augustine, Montaigne, and Woolf. . . . The course is supposed to tackle "the most difficult questions about human experience." . . . In 2015, four Columbia undergraduates wrote an essay in the school newspaper arguing that students "need to feel safe in the classroom" but "many texts in the Western canon" are "wrought with histories and narratives of exclusion and oppression" and contain "triggering and offensive material that marginalizes student identities in the classroom." Some students said that these texts are so emotionally challenging to read and discuss that professors should issue "trigger warnings."[29]

This now happens, and worse. This practice is only intensified on multinational-run social media. Students at universities have become afraid of ideas! Haidt and Lukianoff demonstrate these trends are leading young people to catastrophize, elevate feelings above reality, willfully deny complexity in favor of simplistic binary explanations, irrationally assume they know what people think and their motives, and focus almost exclusively on negatives rather than positives.

As the Western world becomes increasingly sensitive to offense, it is also becoming specifically more offended by the voices of faith, religion, and especially Christianity.

DOES JESUS OFFEND YOU?

When John the Baptist was in prison, he heard about what Jesus was doing and sent his disciples to ask Him, "Are You the Coming One, or are we to look for someone else?" (Matthew 11:3).

Jesus said to them, "Go and report to John what you hear and see: those who are blind receive sight and those who limp walk, those with leprosy are cleansed and those who are deaf hear, the dead are raised, and the poor have the gospel preached to them" (verses 4–5). But then Jesus added, "And blessed is any person who does not take offense at Me" (verse 6).

In Luke we read that when Simeon saw Jesus and his family at the temple in Jerusalem, he blessed them and said to Jesus' mother, Mary, "Behold, this Child is appointed for the fall and rise of many in Israel, and as *a sign to be opposed*" (2:34, emphasis added). Isaiah 8:12–15 also says the Messiah would be a stone of stumbling and a rock of offense.

Are you offended by Jesus?

Most people can cope with the nice-guy Jesus, regardless of whether they profess to be a Christian. They are okay with some bearded guy wandering around Galilee and Jerusalem telling folksy, yet cryptic, morality tales. In Islam they even recognize Jesus as a prophet. The Jews referred to him as a rabbi. He was kind to the poor, the sick, and the outcast. People will even acknowledge He possessed some real wisdom and may even say they try to follow His teachings. That Jesus doesn't offend anybody. So what was Simeon talking about?

When Abbey and Lily were young, they used to go to Build-A-Bear birthday parties at the local mall, where they would make their own custom teddy bear. We can't do this with Jesus. Jesus is not a Build-A-Bear. We can't pick and choose the Jesus that suits our own narrative. He created us, not the other way around (John 1:3). God writes His own narrative, from start to finish. God is the great "I AM." Jesus is the Son of God, the Savior of the world, the Creator of all things, the beginning and the end, the Holy One of God.

What about the Jesus who says He is the only way you can access God and be redeemed for eternity (Mark 16:16; John 3:36; 4:14; 10:27; 12:31–32; 14:6; Acts 4:12)? That's starting to get a bit more uncomfortable. What about the Jesus who says that, excluding Himself, we all have sinned (John 8:29; 15:10; 2 Corinthians 5:21; Hebrews 4:11)? What about the Jesus who says our relationship with a holy God has been broken because He cannot be in a relationship where there is sin (John 5:30; 12:47–48; 15:22)? What about the Jesus who says there is only one way to deal with sin (John 5:27–29; Isaiah 44:22)?

What about the Jesus who says you don't get to redefine what sin is (John 5:22–24; Isaiah 33:22; James 4:12)? Jesus says God's standard is eternal. It is God who decides these things, not the media, not what's trending on Twitter/X, not public opinion, not earthly judges or politicians making laws, not priests or pastors or Christians passing judgment on others. Only God can judge.

What about the Jesus who says you need a Savior to restore your relationship with God because you are a sinner and have fallen short of God's standard (John 6:40; 12:47–48; Romans 3:23)? What about the Jesus who says you can't make things right with God by your own good works, through your own good motives, kindness, or compassion, but only through Him (Matthew 10:32–33; John 12:47–48; Ephesians 2:8–9)? *Well, hang on,* you may now be thinking, *that's not fair. Are you telling me that Jesus says I'm a sinner like everyone else and the only way I can be made right with God is by accepting Jesus as my Savior and accepting His sacrifice for my sin on the cross?* Yes, I am.

C. S. Lewis put it this way: "Either [Jesus] was, and is, the Son of God, or else a madman or something worse. You can shut him up for a fool, you can spit at him and kill him as a demon or you can fall at his feet and call him Lord and God, but let us not come with any patronizing nonsense about his being a great human teacher. He has not left that open to us. He did not intend to."[30]

Now we can start to see what Simeon was talking about when he said Jesus would be a real stumbling block to people wanting to accept and follow Him. If you accept this Jesus, it means you need to change your thinking; you need to be transformed through the renewing of your mind (Romans 12:2) and accept some hard truths about your own self. This is very inconvenient.

It is also true that when Christians truly live out their faith in Jesus, including living out the love for others that Jesus commands, they are likely to cause offense for the same reason Jesus does, and will suffer as a result. In Richard Stearns's book *The Hole in Our Gospel*, he reminds us that "those who choose to follow Christ have struggled since the very beginning to live differently in a world that often rejects their values and mocks their beliefs."[31] When we love God and allow Him to transform our lives, we will also offend this world, and it will become difficult to live in.

As the Western world becomes more secular, we can expect the public expression and practice of our Christian faith to come under increasing challenge. It has already begun. We will likely face increased discrimination, marginalization, and even persecution. A once-dominant Christian culture in the West has become a minority culture. But that does not mean it is a defeated culture. Remember, "we are more than conquerors" (Romans 8:37 NIV).

The church in the former Soviet Union knew all about this, and so does today's church in communist China or Iran. The church has always flourished under persecution. Perhaps that is what is occurring in the West. How often have you heard sermons and prayers calling for revival? Perhaps God has a different idea of how this is going to be realized. Perhaps God is waking us out of our comfort zone.

Jesus was way ahead of this. In Matthew 10:16–18 we read His instructions to His disciples when He sent them out into the world. He said, "Behold, I am sending you out as sheep in the midst of wolves; so be as wary as serpents, and as innocent as doves. But be on guard against people, for they will hand you over to the courts and flog you in their synagogues; and you will even be brought before governors and kings on My account, as a testimony to them and to the Gentiles." He then reminded us in Matthew 10:32–33, "Therefore, everyone who confesses Me before people, I will also confess him before My Father who is in heaven. But whoever denies Me before people, I will also deny him before My Father who is in heaven."

So yes, we should continue to be bold in the confession of our faith and not be intimidated by the secularization of our society that will increasingly oppress Christians. We should not be silent about it, but we should also be smart about it. We must be as wary as serpents and innocent as doves. We must also remember it is Christ who is the rock of offense, not you. Being offensive is not proof of being spiritual. Sometimes it is just proof of being obnoxious.

The only offense that others should see in Christians is the evidence of God's positive impact on our lives. Love, joy, peace, patience, kindness, goodness, faithfulness, gentleness, and self-control—this is the evidence that Paul talked about (Galatians 5:22–23).

Rod Dreher observes in *The Benedict Option* that "Christians didn't ask for internal exile from a country we thought was our own, but that's where we find ourselves. We are a minority now, so let's be a creative one, offering warm, living, light-filled alternatives to a world growing cold, dead, and dark."[32] He makes a good point.

LESSONS FROM OUR FAILURE

It is true that much of the West's rejection of God can be boiled down to the desire for people to become their own god, the influences of popular culture, the media, technology, and increasingly secular parliaments changing laws to reflect new prevailing moral sentiments. However, we should not gloss over what this rapid secularization says about the failure of the Christian witness in Western society, especially since the end of the Second World War.

Significant and terrible events have seriously undermined the effectiveness of the church's institutional witness in modern Western society, and we must acknowledge, confront, repent of, seek forgiveness for, and overcome these in Jesus' name. The most significant has been the abominable revelations of sexual abuse, including of children in Christian religious institutions.

A bipartisan Royal Commission initiated by one of my predecessors, Labor prime minister Julia Gillard, into institutional child sex abuse revealed an appalling record of despicable offenses taking place over decades.[33] These offenses were not limited to Christian organizations. Sexual predators respect no barriers and seek opportunity for their depraved obsessions wherever they can find it. Government agencies, charitable institutions, and youth organizations, just like the church, have all played host to these predators and, sadly, have even protected them.

When Dad was running a youth program for boys at our local church, called Boys' Brigade, he was occasionally approached by men who wanted to volunteer. As a police officer, Dad would never just accept things at face value. He'd seen too much. These days there are thankfully all sorts of background checks that must be passed before people can work with children. Back then, such checks did not exist, so Dad took it on himself and did his own unofficial research at work to ensure the boys he was responsible for were protected. I'm very grateful he did. I wish more leaders had been able to do the same.

As prime minister, I led the government's response to the Royal Commission's findings, delivered the national apology to victims in our Parliament as recommended by the Royal Commission, and implemented the National Redress Scheme.[34] I will never forget the day of the national apology. I had previously spent time meeting with survivors and their advocacy groups because I knew just how important this apology and speech would be to them. They had been waiting their entire lives for the acknowledgment of what had been done to them. I wanted them to know that their cries had been heard and believed and that redress would be provided, demonstrating accountability for what was done to them.

After delivering the apology in the parliamentary chamber, I walked into the Great Hall of our Parliament to address the survivors who had come to Canberra for the occasion. I had never been in a room filled with so many wounded and broken people. As I read out the official apology proclamation, I invited those on the platform, including the leader of the opposition, Bill Shorten, to join hands with me. All others in the room did the same. In my own mind I was praying furiously for the Holy Spirit to bring peace to the room as I could sense an intense spiritual battle raging. I had been very conscious of this spiritual environment the minute I stepped into the room.

Afterward, I walked out onto the lawns of Parliament House where more survivors had gathered. I listened to their stories. There were hugs, tears, and also a few smiles. Among the crowd I met an old school friend of mine. The hurt among those who were there was palpable. It was emotionally exhausting.

As I walked back toward Parliament I took the unusual step

of calling Bill and requested that we not hold "question time" that day—the period when the opposing parties would typically debate each other on the issues of the day. To his credit, Bill readily agreed. This was not a day for combative politics; it was a day for peace and healing. Bill had similar experiences to mine in his own interactions that day. Not only would the regular political jousting take away from the significant events of the day, but frankly I was in no state to enter the chamber and engage in such activity. I returned to my office, shut the door behind me, put my head in my hands, and wept and prayed for all those whose lives had been shattered by this evil.

This failure of the Christian church in Western society, both by its institutions and by its individual members, had shattered public trust. As a result, an institution that was once seen as an enormous positive influence on society was now undermined. Christians were just as disgusted as those outside the church and were equally scathing of the perpetrators and those who sought to cover up their egregious crimes. And while the overwhelming majority of Christian churches and organizations had no part in these terrible events, widespread damage was nevertheless inflicted on the entire Christian church's reputation. The far greater damage was to the victims who found abuse where they should have found safety and love. Other high-profile moral and governance failures of church leaders have also served to exacerbate cynicism and distrust of organized Christianity.

I was therefore not surprised when I recently read an opinion article in Australia's national newspaper by a left-wing journalist. In her piece she asserted, "It feels like there's no exchange of embracing love in these arch conservative religious movements. Just an erecting of walls. To keep people out. Many young people look on in bewilderment and revulsion at values not of their world. They champion qualities like kindness, tolerance, equality and fairness.

Yet do modern church movements . . . embody these? No wonder so many young people don't define themselves as religious anymore— yet may see themselves as spiritual."[35]

I don't believe the writer's assessment can be fairly applied to the broad expanse of evangelical churches in Australia or elsewhere, certainly not my own in Sutherland. I also suspect there is some prejudice behind it, but that's not the point. The article provides an insight into the thinking of those who know what fruit a church should bear and aren't seeing it anymore. How can we have allowed our Christian faith, authored by the God of love, to be seen as loveless? That said, we will not find the answer to that question in the hostile commentary of our secular critics, who demand that we simply conform to their new secular order.

Some churches have done this and chosen to address these per-ceptions by just becoming a dull copy of "progressive" society in order to seek public acceptance. If you can't beat them, join them. Many liberal churches have gone down this path for many years. They have become tepid and conformed to the deep secularist values that dominate their communities, and they are dying as a result. That is not the answer. These churches are inoffensive for all the wrong reasons. They have embraced "the gods of the people of the land," which Joshua warned Israel about (Joshua 23:6–7).

As Christians, our response to a world and a society that are increasingly offended by Jesus and rejecting God must be to hold firm to the confession of our faith and to hope without wavering. Most importantly, hope and love must be evident in our own lives. This will only occur to the extent that we put Christ at the center of our lives and allow Him to transform us by embracing His gospel and returning to the fundamentals of our faith.

Such transformation means living out the blessing of God by being a blessing to others. We are blessed to be a blessing. It's about being the hands and feet of Christ in a hurting world, in our neighborhoods and local communities, both individually and corporately. It's about loving your neighbor and even loving and forgiving your enemies. Your neighbors may not be too convinced about the integrity of the Christian church more broadly, but make sure that your witness and actions as a Christian are positive, and let your prayer be that they can see Christ in you. Let that be the only offense anyone is likely to see in you, and let that also be the prayer of your local church.

Chapter Five

ARE YOU STRONG ENOUGH?

He gives strength to the weary, and to the one
who lacks might He increases power.
ISAIAH 40:29

I remember the first time I saw the Oscar-winning film *Chariots of Fire*.[1] Mum and Dad took me and my brother, Alan, to an old theater called the Randwick Ritz in the eastern suburbs of Sydney, where we grew up. Unlike today's modern cinemas with their digital sound systems, reclining seats, and molded cup holders, this was an old-fashioned theatre. The screen was erected on a theatre stage, with long, red draped curtains on either side. We sat on the old leather seats on the upstairs balcony where the springs in the upholstery seemed to have a life of their own. I was thirteen years old.

I was captivated and inspired by the story of Scottish sprinter Eric Liddell at the Paris Olympics of 1924. I particularly loved one beautiful scene where Eric and his sister, Jennie, are in the countryside after a church service. The sun is setting behind them. Jennie is frustrated that Eric is spending all his time training for the Olympics and neglecting his ministry calling to serve God as a missionary in China. Eric knew that China would one day be his mission, but he also knew the other calling God had placed on his life. In what has become one of the most beloved lines of the famous film, Eric explains to his devoted sister, "Jennie, you've got to understand. I believe that God made me for a purpose. For China. But He also made me fast. And when I run, I feel His pleasure." What could be more important than that?

When we worship God it brings Him great pleasure (Hebrews 13:15–16). Our worship is not just in the praises we sing or the prayers we offer. It is the sacrifice of living out our gifting and purpose in life that God equipped us to perform. God takes delight in each of us. Remember that He said we are fearfully and wonderfully made (Psalm 139:14). Which of us, after completing a minor building project, or making a delicious meal, or even after cleaning out the garage or mowing the lawn, has not just stepped back to appreciate it? We are made in God's image. God delights in His creation, which means He takes delight in you. Nothing delights God more than His relationship with you and strengthening you to be all He created you to be.

God does not want to be a passive bystander in our lives. It's not like He just brought us into being and said, "Well, good luck with that. I've done My part. I'll see you on the other side. I hope you make it." We do not worship or serve a disinterested God. To the contrary, God created us to have relationship with Him every single day we draw breath. It is for this purpose that God sent the Holy Spirit. Jesus said, "I will ask the Father, and He will give you another Helper, so that He may be with you forever" (John

We are made in God's image. God delights in His creation, which means He takes delight in you.

14:16) and, "The Spirit of truth . . . will guide you into all the truth" (16:13).

Nothing brings God greater delight than seeing His plans and purposes realized for you (Jeremiah 29:11). And nothing energizes and constantly refreshes you more than being in the center of His will. I pray that this is something you have experienced in your life. I have. When you know you are truly acting out God's presence and plans in your life, you are able to experience the witness of the Holy Spirit with your own spirit. It can be anything from showing the simplest kindness to a stranger to incredible feats of human achievement—from teaching a child how to read, to making a meal for your neighbor, to securing the release of one of your citizens who had been wrongly imprisoned by the Iranian government (which I had some experience with as PM). God's smile is as great for each of them. Nothing beats that.

The good news is that whatever path God's plan for our good takes us down, no matter how demanding, how frustrating, or how exhausting, God will always ensure we have the strength to bear it. He will renew our strength and enable us to rise to His purposes as the occasion demands. He will supply the courage, the peace, the rest, the energy, the wisdom, the patience, or whatever else it takes to enable us to keep to that path.

> *The good news is that whatever path God's plan for our good takes us down, He will always ensure we have the strength to bear it.*

In another scene from *Chariots of Fire*, Eric is preaching to a crowd after an athletics meet. Liddell says, "You came to see a race today. See someone win. Happened to be me." The crowd laughs as the rain begins pouring down on them. "Where does the power come from to see the race to its end?" he asks. "From within." He goes on to quote Jesus: "Behold, the kingdom of God is within you. . . . If, with all your hearts ye truly seek Me, ye shall ever surely find Me" (Luke

17:21; Jeremiah 29:13). Liddell concludes by saying, "That is how you run the straight race."

A PILGRIMAGE

In April 2009, I joined a trekking group to walk the Kokoda Trail in Papua New Guinea. The trail is a 125-kilometer trek (or 80 miles) across the rugged, mountainous jungle of the Owen Stanley Range, just north of Port Moresby. It is an Australian pilgrimage. The backstory to this journey began before I entered politics.

In December 2005, the peace of our southern suburbs of the Shire was shattered by an outbreak of ugly hatred and violence. There had been a series of scuffles between local lifeguards on our beach and visitors. The locals were largely Anglo-Australians and the visitors were Middle Eastern–background Muslim Australians. One particular day the lifeguards took issue with the visiting youths kicking footballs on the beach without any consideration for others and behaving inappropriately toward some of the girls on the beach. The lifeguards called out this behavior and were then assaulted by the visitors. This did not go down well with the locals. It wasn't the first time there had been tensions between the two groups. What had already been brewing finally boiled over. What followed over the next few days tore at the fabric of Australia's multicultural society.

An angry mob of around five thousand people, some fueled by alcohol, dressed in national flags, gathered en masse in the park by the beach. Many were from outside the area. As is often the case in such gatherings, the more extreme participants took over. The crowd started to chant racist and anti-Muslim slogans. The situation quickly spiraled out of control. Many who attended that day would not have imagined being part of an angry riot. That is not why they came, and many who came refused to participate in this behavior, but it still happened. It was ugly. The images went around the world. I was in Dubai at the time on business for Tourism Australia and saw the international reports. People of Muslim and Middle Eastern appearance were targeted by the mob, including as they sat on a train stationed at the platform. Brave police and good-natured locals sought to shield those who were being attacked. These were Australians attacking Australians on our own streets in one of the most peaceful suburbs of Sydney.

More shame would follow as revenge attacks were carried out, including against one local young Anglo-Australian man in the Shire. Middle Eastern attackers from outside the area randomly set upon him in the parking lot of a local golf course and stabbed him. Across the bay from the Shire, Middle Eastern mobs attacked Anglo-Australians on the streets. One Middle Eastern youth climbed the flagpole of the local Returned Services League (RSL) building, took down the Australian flag, and burned it. After several days police restored order and the local community leaders began the process of confronting the nasty tension that had been lurking below the surface for some time. What became clear was that these communities knew nothing about each other and had little respect for each other.

Our local volunteer surf lifesaving clubs in the Shire decided to do something positive about it. They would invite young people of Middle Eastern Muslim backgrounds from outside the area to join their club and become trained lifeguards. The program proved to be a great success in breaking down barriers.

One of the young women who accepted the invitation turned up in what she described as her burkini, marrying her religious culture with her newfound passion to become a volunteer lifeguard. She was making an important statement that her religion and culture were as much a part of Australia as any other. She was also saying that she wanted her culture to embrace being part of Australia and not be separate from it.

When I became the local member of Parliament for the Shire, I wanted to continue this work. One evening I was watching a news magazine program called *Compass*.[2] In this program we were introduced to the young man who had scaled the RSL flagpole and the extraordinary veterans at the RSL who had chosen not to condemn the young man but rather to engage him. They had arranged for him to undertake a trek in Papua New Guinea along the Kokoda Trail.

The Kokoda Trail was the scene of one of Australia's fiercest and bravest battles during World War II. In 1942, Australian soldiers repelled Japanese troops advancing across the Owen Stanley Range toward Port Moresby. At that time this was Australian territory. The Kokoda Trail campaign was a nation-shaping event, like the ANZAC assault on Gallipoli during the First World War.

The RSL veterans wanted to find a way to help the young man see how he was a beneficiary of the sacrifices the soldiers had made on that bloody and awful trail. They wanted to find a way for him to understand that he was included, not excluded. Those brave men had made the ultimate sacrifice for the future of Australia, and this young man was part of that future. The veterans rightly assumed that the young man had felt no connection with the stories of our country or how they were relevant to him. They understood that he was angry, hurt, and wanted to lash out. Rather than judging him, they chose to try to break down some barriers and build some understanding. They gave up their justifiable right to be offended and chose to restore. They arranged for the young man to travel to Papua New Guinea and trek the Kokoda Trail.

The *Compass* episode, called "Cronulla to Kokoda," followed his trek through the jungle. It's a really tough trek, usually taking about six to eight days. The terrain is very steep and arduous, and when the rain comes down it can be impossible. This is enough to break anyone down. And so it happened for this young man. In his physical and mental exhaustion he broke down and realized that what he had done was in ignorance and anger and that there was a better way forward. When he returned home, the RSL veterans invited him to march alongside them and carry the Australian national flag at the annual Anzac Day march to honor our veterans, like Memorial Day in the United States. It was a great honor and a wonderful story of reconciliation and restoration.

When I saw the program I realized this was something that we had to replicate. I contacted my federal parliamentary colleague Jason Clare, who was the new Labor MP for Blaxland, an area where there was a large Middle Eastern Muslim community. We had both just been elected to the federal Parliament. We'd already been talking about a bipartisan approach to mending relations between our two communities following the riots and revenge attacks. We agreed we would lead a trek across Kokoda, taking a total of ten young men and women from each of our communities. We called it the Mateship Trek. We were joined by a local doctor, Jamal Rifi, and a local school principal, Jihad Dibb. We all became good friends. The trek would be a demonstration of healing and understanding between the young people of our communities.

In the months ahead we trained hard and raised sponsorship to be able to undertake the trek. For six and a half days we trudged along the trail, starting the day after Anzac Day. It was the hardest thing I've ever done. For about eight to ten hours a day we scaled steep ascents only to reach the summit and then struggled to avoid sliding down the other side, sometimes in the pouring rain.

The Kokoda trek pushed us to our physical limits. We knew we either had to break through or break down. To make it through, we paid close attention to our physical well-being. We looked after our feet and kept ourselves hydrated and fueled. On the first night a young man named Matt who worked in my office from the Shire was so exhausted from the first day's climb that he went straight to bed when the camp was set up and missed the evening meal. We hadn't noticed. The next night as we scaled the top of Ioribaiwa Ridge, Matt collapsed at the summit. This was serious. Numerous Australians have died from exhaustion or misadventure while undertaking this trek. In fact, alongside where he collapsed there was a memorial to a trekker who had died on that very spot. Just prior to our departing, there had been two deaths on the trail. The local trek guides attended to Matt with great skill and care. After spending a long time recovering at the top of the ridge, Matt was assisted down to camp. The next day he had to be evacuated by helicopter. His tank was empty. His strength was gone, and it could not be restored in time to carry on with the trek.

While attending to our physical well-being was incredibly important, much of the challenge was in our heads. We had to stay positive and keep looking forward, taking one step at a time. As we walked the trail, our guide shared the stories of the horrendous battles that had taken place where our footsteps were now leaving their impressions in the mud. We were inspired. Their stories were the stuff of legend.

On the northern side of the Owen Stanley Range, there is a small village known as Isurava that looks down on the village of Kokoda on the floodplain below. Isurava was the location of one of the fiercest battles during the campaign. On the battle site there is a magnificent Australian memorial to our soldiers with four stone pillars standing guard. A word is engraved on each of these pillars: *Courage, Mateship, Endurance, Sacrifice*. At this memorial we held a commemoration service to honor all those who had sacrificed their lives for Australia's freedom. I laid a wreath for Sergeant Brett Till. It was incredibly moving.

A strong bond formed among the trekking group, and it became important to each of us that we all get through. It was not uncommon that when the stronger trekkers would get into camp they would drop their packs and head back up the ridge to help the others down to camp. We looked out for each other. Up on the trail it no longer mattered which group we had come from; we were all one, and that sense enabled us to get to the end and learn some really important lessons. Any differences we may have perceived at the start of the trek had vanished. We drew strength from one another. In many ways we became stronger each day as our physical exhaustion increased. Yes, we were tired, cramped, blistered, and sore, but we had been able to discover a strength beyond ourselves that enabled us to endure to the end of the trail.

When we returned to Port Moresby we visited the Bomana War Cemetery, where we stood together holding hands and facing the graves of the more than two thousand soldiers buried there. We each made a commitment to live a life worthy of their sacrifice, which included recognizing that they had given their lives for Australia's future, which was now us. It was up to us to get it right and do the best we could, just as the soldiers on the Kokoda Trail campaign had endeavored to do with the challenges they'd faced. They had sacrificed their tomorrows for our today.

LIKE EAGLES

When I became prime minister, I would often think back to my time trekking through the jungle and apply the lessons I learned about endurance along the trail: focusing on what was most important,

91

drawing on those around me, and most of all looking beyond myself for the strength that was needed. However, politics is no brief trek in the jungle. We were facing extraordinary challenges as a nation, with the lives of tens of thousands at stake. In these circumstances, I got on my knees and looked to God for strength.

While the job of serving as prime minister was a difficult one, living with difficulty is not unique to national leaders. This is true for most people contending with life's challenges—a parent raising a child, a family running its local small business, or worse, people whose homes have been burned to the ground in a bushfire or washed away in a flood or who are struggling with a terrible illness or are caring for someone who is.

We all can become exhausted by life. We can also lose hope when weariness overwhelms us. I've felt this way on many occasions and used strategies for coping with physical and mental stress. I took up lap swimming. I would read and go for walks. I also kept up my passion for cooking curries from scratch, losing myself for several hours, invariably leaving behind an apocalyptic mess in the kitchen. Whatever you choose to do, the key is finding something to immerse yourself in so you can switch off and think about something else.

All of this is fine and good, but these things do not give you the spiritual strength you need to walk the path that God has set before you. This is where my faith life was transformational. As a Christian, I was able to draw on a strength beyond myself. Were it not for the sustaining presence of God, I never would have survived as long as I did in so many high offices. I've also been blessed by the wonderful people God put in my life to help sustain me, particularly my family and friends. But most of all I needed God.

About a month before the 2019 election, I was exhausted and somewhat despondent. We were continuing to trail in the polls and time was running out. I was on my way to the Central Coast of New

South Wales just north of Sydney for a campaign rally. Jen was with me. I had recently shared with my pastor friends in our chat group how I had been reaching for God but not really feeling His presence. He seemed distant to me. I just wanted to know that He was with me in all of this. Of course I wanted to win, but what was more important to me was His presence, His peace, and His assurance. I knew I could not function without these.

Before arriving at an event, we would typically go to a holding location to give time for media and security to be in place at the venue. On this occasion we stopped off at the Ken Duncan Gallery. Ken is a famous Australian photographer known for his inspirational Australian landscape and wildlife portraits. Ken is also a strong Christian. His images are incredible acts of worship. I walked into the side room of the gallery on my own. I really needed a lift and was reaching out to God once more.

There I was confronted by the majestic image of an eagle in full flight, with the wind beneath its wings, that Ken had taken on an expedition to Finland. The detail in the photograph was extraordinary. I stood there transfixed, stunned into silence by its majesty. The image was titled *Soaring Majesty*. Isaiah 40:31 rushed into my mind.

> Yet those who wait for the LORD
> Will gain new strength;
> They will mount up with wings like eagles,
> They will run and not get tired,
> They will walk and not become weary.

I strongly sensed God's presence right there in that room with me. He was reminding me where my strength would come from and that He was indeed with me, no matter what.

I bought the print and hung it in my study in the Kirribilli residence, where it remained for the next three years after we won the election. Each day I was there, I would look at it and be reminded of God's presence and faithfulness. He would always be with me.

We can be confident that when we wait on God to renew our strength, it will be there when we need it, but we have to move to know it and receive it.

When I was prime minister, I recounted this story in an address to a national conference of evangelical pastors on the Gold Coast in Queensland. It was a large gathering. I'm not sure they had ever heard a prime minister preach before. I chose to tell this story of my visit to Ken Duncan's gallery as a witness to God's goodness and faithfulness in my life but also because there was a further truth behind it that I wanted to share.

In the verses I noticed that those who had waited for the Lord discovered their strength had been renewed only after they had moved. They realized they did not get tired until they had run, they did not become weary until they had walked, and they did not find their wings until they had mounted up. We can be confident that when we wait on God to renew our strength, it will be there when we need it, but we have to move to know it and receive it. Only when you move will you feel His power. Only when you run, walk, and mount up will you find God's strength kicking in. This is what we are called to, moving forward in the knowledge that God will always be the source of our strength. Eric Liddell was right—God is where the power comes from.

SOURCES OF STRENGTH

Joshua was someone who knew where his strength came from. So did Moses. God taught them both that they could not run their race alone.

In Exodus 17:8–14 we read the story of Moses ordering Joshua to pick some men to go and fight against the Amalekites, who had picked a fight with Israel. When Joshua went out to battle, Moses would go and stand on top of the hill holding "the staff of God." The next day, as the battle was raging, whenever Moses raised his hands, Israel prevailed, but whenever he lowered his hands, Amalek gained the advantage. The problem was that Moses was getting tired. So they got a stone for him to sit on, while his brother, Aaron, and another man named Hur held up his hands, one on each side. Thankfully, Moses's hands were now able to remain steady until the end of the day, and Joshua won the battle.

I have always liked this story. One of the most frequent requests I made of my pastors' group was that they "hold up their staff" in prayer as I went about the battle on the ground below.

It is pure vanity to think we can achieve the purposes of God in our own strength. There is no doubt that Joshua was a great warrior and incredibly impressive in battle. He would have been greatly admired by his soldiers and the people of Israel for his bravery and leadership on the battlefield. Perhaps some even thought Joshua should be their leader and not Moses.

What is first evident from this account and so many others is that Joshua did not, as we say in Australia, have "tickets on himself," which means he was not excessively proud of himself, or vain. He understood that all his victories belonged to God. Joshua also understood his part in God's process. He knew he was part of a hierarchy established by God where authority had been provided for Moses to lead the

It is pure vanity to think we can achieve the purposes of God in our own strength.

way to the promised land. Joshua respected and honored Moses's authority. He didn't get big ideas about himself. He didn't complain about why he had to go and fight while Moses and his mates went and sat up on the hill, muttering something about holding up a stick. Moses gave Joshua his marching orders, and off he would go. Joshua understood his duty and performed it so faithfully that when the time came to enter the promised land, God raised him to lead the nation after Moses passed on.

Second, the story is a reminder of how God wants us all to play a role in His purposes. There is a bit of the theater of the absurd in this story. Moses keeps his staff up and Joshua prevails; he drops his staff and the battle turns against Joshua. It hardly seems fair. What possible effect was there in the raising of Moses's staff? About the same as when he raised it to part the Red Sea or struck the rock to bring forth water, I suppose. Once again it was an act of obedience, an act of faith. Of greater significance was the recognition of their reliance on God's strength to deliver the battle, but they also had agency in this. They had to do their part.

We can't just sit back and expect God to do all the work and see the blessings flow. Our relationship with God is not passive, and it is not one-way. God expects us to get involved and have skin in the game. When Isaiah said our strength is renewed as we wait on the Lord, he was not talking about us passively checking out. It is actually during our times of waiting that we pray our most earnest prayers. These are the times when God often draws us closest. These are the times when we seek Him most desperately and when He strengthens us for the race or climb or flight ahead. This preparation is important. So when you find yourself in the middle of following that new job cross-country or raising kids or launching a new business or following up on that doctor's visit or dealing with a national crisis, you are well prepared by the God who was with you during your time of waiting. We'll talk more about this in chapter 9 ("Why Are You Waiting?"). Whether we are in the waiting or in the walking, we must never be passive in our relationship with God. He is always expecting there to be a voice at the other end of the line.

The third lesson is that even the great Moses needed to lean on others who God had put around him to help him keep his staff in the air. If they hadn't stepped up, the whole enterprise would have failed. It took more than Joshua's bravery and Moses's faith. Moses had his own physical limitations. It was the same when we walked Kokoda. If one of us failed in our strength, we would rely on those with us to help bring us through. We must be conscious of those God puts around us.

Our relationship with God is not passive, and it is not one-way. God expects us to get involved and have skin in the game.

As Christians we should never diminish the important role we each need to play in the work of God to renew our strength by supporting one another. I will be forever grateful for the blessing of my own local church at Horizon during the challenging years of my time in politics. Their prayers, support, and encouragement were amazing. The instruction, wisdom, and practical support from our pastoral team, led by Brad Bonhomme and previously Michael Murphy, were also a real blessing. We were also encouraged by the large number of Christians who I know prayed for me and my family every day. As often as I would come under attack, I would also receive letter after letter and message after message from Christians across the country and even overseas who were raising their voices in prayer.

We are all the body of Christ. It is God's purpose that we be proactively engaged in His plans and purposes. God acts through the body of Christ, His church. He established the church for a reason. We are all part of it, and we must attend to it. We must nurture it, we must cherish it, and, where necessary, we must defend it.

We should also not pretend we can do without it, as some are in the habit of doing these days (Hebrews 10:25). I am always saddened when I hear people say they love Jesus and have their own relationship with God but don't see the need to be part of any church. The body of Christ is a great and important blessing in itself, and we are meant to be a blessing to others in that fellowship. Church is not just about what we receive. We must be mindful that we are not created to walk our faith journey alone. The source of our strength is of course God, but He so often chooses to renew our strength through the actions and love of His church. You cannot expect to live a life of faith in the blessings of God if you cut yourself off from one of the very channels through which God delivers His blessings to you. The body of Christ in action is an incredible force. We should not underestimate our role in it nor the role it plays in renewing our strength and transforming our societies.

RIDING THE UPDRAFTS

The good gifts God places in our lives are there to reassure us of His presence and to equip and strengthen us when trials are upon us. The more we acknowledge them and give thanks for them, the greater impact these blessings have in our lives. When things are not going as we want them to, we usually find time to let God know all about it. And that's okay. He wants us to talk to Him about it. But perhaps our perspective on the negative events in our lives would be different if we were also in the habit of appreciating the many blessings that were intended to better equip us for the very trials we are now experiencing.

When you are blessed with good health, praise God. When you experience the encouragement of a true friend, praise God. When you hear a word in season from your pastor or the revelation of Scripture in your morning reading, praise God. When you see an answer to prayer, praise God. When you reflect on the knowledge that God listens to our prayers, praise God. When you enjoy the smile and laughter of your children, praise God. When you receive the patience, intimacy, and love of your wife or husband, praise God.

For my dog Buddy's wagging tail and enthusiastic greeting at the end of a hard day, I praise God. For a great curry on a Saturday night with all the family around the table, I praise God. I have even been known to praise God when my team, the Sharks, wins on the weekend.

Our trials and challenges come as no surprise to God. By acknowledging, articulating, and giving thanks for God's blessings in our lives, no matter how small or how great, we familiarize our-selves with the tools and supports that God has put around us to strengthen us when the occasion requires it. We tip the balance of our consciousness toward the positive agency of God in our lives, enabling us to walk confidently in His favor, regardless of the circumstances.

Jesus plainly said, "In the world you have tribulation, but take courage; I have overcome the world" (John 16:33). Despondency, oppression, disappointment, discouragement, frustration—each of these can weigh us down. They can crush our hope if we permit them to. It would be wrong to think that these things are not real; they are. The loss of a job, the sickness of a child, the death of a parent, a failed marriage, the dissolution of a business, the bullying of your friends at school or online, the loss of an election—the impact of these events is real. Knowing God intends good plans for us does not mean these hard things won't happen to us. They will and do. We may never know victory in the way the world defines it, but we

> *By acknowledging, articulating, and giving thanks for God's blessings in our lives, we familiarize ourselves with the tools and supports that God has put around us to strengthen us.*

can be assured of His victory. Remember Stephen's beaming face as he confronted his own brutal death by stoning (Acts 7:54–56).

It is also true that such events can actually be beyond our human ability to cope. What a reassurance then from Isaiah that God knows it will require His agency to enable us to rise and not be pressed down by the forces of disappointment and discouragement. In life there are updrafts and downdrafts. The downdrafts are those forces that come against us and can crush our spirits and steal our hope. The updrafts come from God. Isaiah says, "Those who wait for the LORD will renew their strength" and "mount up with wings like eagles." Eagles soar as the air rises beneath their wings. It is a powerful image: you stretch out your wings, completely vulnerable and reliant on God to provide the updraft. It can be a bold and frightening thing to do. Standing there, your wings outstretched, your undercarriage exposed. Why would you do it? Because you are mindful of the arc of God's faithfulness throughout your life, you know that you can trust Him. So you stretch out your wings in faith, you wait on Him in faith, and you mount up and soar as He has promised.

Chapter Six

WHY DO YOU WORRY?

Do not be anxious about anything, but in everything
by prayer and pleading with thanksgiving let your
requests be made known to God. And the peace
of God, which surpasses all comprehension, will
guard your hearts and minds in Christ Jesus.
PHILIPPIANS 4:6–7

In the film *Bridge of Spies*, Tom Hanks plays a lawyer, James
Donovan, who chooses to defend an alleged Russian spy in
America during the Cold War.[1] The charge of espionage carries
the death penalty. Despite his personal misgivings about his client's
alleged crimes, Donovan believes that an accused person should
receive a fair trial and a competent legal defense. This is founda-
tional to the rule of law that underpins our freedom in Western
democracies. Rather than being seen as a patriot, Donovan is sadly
branded a traitor and ostracized in the climate of Cold War America

in the 1960s. Mark Rylance, a brilliant British actor, plays the alleged spy, Rudolf Abel.

Abel is being held in prison. He is sitting in an interview room with Donovan, who explains to Abel that, as his attorney, he will be the only one in his corner. He says, "Quite frankly, everybody else has an interest in sending you to the electric chair."

Abel looks back at him blankly and says, "All right."

An awkward silence ensues. Perplexed, Donovan finally inquires, "You don't seem alarmed?"

Abel shrugs his shoulders and calmly says, "Would it help?"

During the COVID-19 pandemic, there was a lot I could have worried about as prime minister, but like Rudolf Abel, I was deeply aware that worrying would not help. Prayer was helpful, yes; and there was plenty of it. But worry, no. In late March 2020, I confided in my pastors' chat group, "It constantly feels like you have just come back up [for air] after diving under a huge wave [in the surf] to see another 5 [waves], in the set bigger than the last. . . . I just pray that I can cushion the blow for as many as possible and just bring us all through."

In existential situations like this, politics and ideology do not matter. I wasn't dealing with a political conspiracy; I was dealing with a biological pathogen. I focused on the things I could do something about and then tried to get as much information as I could on the things we didn't yet know anything about. I also did all I could to bring and hold people together. The country needed unity, not division. As the national leader, I was the one who had to make the political sacrifices to make that happen. If that meant I had to take a political hit and bear the brunt of the criticism and blame in order to keep the team together, then that was my job. That's what leadership required, and I accepted the consequences.

In crises like these, there are always some people who will talk endlessly about the problem. Others will stand back and criticize. Then there are those who will seek to take political advantage and undermine you for their own political gain. I encountered them all. Thankfully, I also had ministers and officials who wanted to help me solve problems—in particular, Deputy Prime Minister Michael McCormack, Treasurer Josh Frydenberg, and Health Minister Greg Hunt.

RESPONDING TO COVID

In early 2020, at the outset of the pandemic, we were advised by our health experts and officials that Australia could be facing the loss of fifty thousand lives. To put this in some perspective, thirty-four thousand Australian lives were lost in World War II. We now knew we were facing the most significant challenge since that era. Politics no longer mattered. This was about Australia's survival. We had to get Australia through. We saw the horror show unfolding in some of the most developed nations and cities in the world. New York, London, Rome, Paris—they were falling like dominoes.

Late one night, early in the pandemic, I returned home to The Lodge in Canberra and was watching an overseas special news report where they had been able to film inside one of the chaotic COVID emergency wards of a hospital in northern Italy. The camera panned down a corridor crowded with gurneys carrying patients gasping for air. They then entered a room full of patients fighting for their lives with the few respirators the hospital had available. The image was horrifying. I turned to Jen and said, "This is just awful. This could happen here if we don't get this right." I continued, "But imagine how much worse it's going to be when this virus hits Indonesia and other countries that won't have the health system or resources to fight it that we do. They will just be laying the bodies out in the village streets—no one will ever know just how many people this thing will kill." I was determined to do whatever I had to do to prevent a repeat of the terrible scenes we were seeing overseas.

The pandemic was now unfolding in real time. No one was making this up. The corpses piling up and the mass graves were not lying. People were dying horrible deaths in large numbers all around the world. More deaths would follow—often lonely deaths, separated from loved ones, who would also then be forced to grieve alone. It was heartbreaking. At the start of the pandemic, no one knew how deadly this virus was. In Australia we had a different take on COVID-19 than many countries in the Northern Hemisphere, including the United States. This may explain why our populations reacted differently. Like many countries in Asia, we had seen the SARS and MERS pandemics back in 2002 and 2012, respectively. Our concern was that this virus might be just as deadly but even harder to contain. There was no vaccine, and one had never been developed for this type of virus before. We had no idea how long it would take to create one. We didn't really know how the virus spread. We didn't even know if you could get it twice. There were few weapons to fight this thing, so we had to use the measures available to us, as objectionable as they might have been. Again, we had to focus on the things we knew and the things we could do, not the things we didn't know and couldn't influence.

Every day and all day, from early in the morning until late into the evening, I met with our various teams working on different aspects of our response. One of our earliest actions was to get Australians out of Wuhan, China. Brave consular officials from our Department of Foreign Affairs jumped in a car and made their way to Wuhan to organize the uplift. I called the CEO of Qantas, our national airline, and asked him to organize flights to get our people out. He didn't hesitate.

Every day involved making a large number of decisions. On each occasion I assumed the best about Australians, that if we backed them with the decisions we made, they would have the good sense, patience, courage, resilience, and kindness needed to get through. I was not disappointed.

I also worked to establish backup plans in case a cabinet member came down with the virus. I ensured we put appropriate checks and balances on the extraordinary powers, established by activating our Biosecurity Act and the extraordinary financial delegations we now had at our disposal. Throughout the course of the pandemic, I ensured we had a parliamentary committee conducting an ongoing inquiry to our national COVID-19 response. This committee had the authority to call witnesses and get explanations from officials for all the decisions and actions being taken. Our health response, our economic response, our industry response, and many more targeted lines of effort all had teams working on them and reporting back into our National Security Committee, which I chaired.

As we managed this crisis, it was essential to ensure we were all working off the same information. From the outset I insisted on a daily report with a common data set that was authoritatively sourced and regularly updated. Every new insight that our teams picked up from overseas and within Australia was critical to informing the decisions we had to make. It covered everything from financial data to daily case numbers, hospitalizations, deaths, calls to mental health helplines, and so much more. Bond issuance clearance rates were especially critical as they would determine the scale of response we could afford. We operated at a level of intensity that I doubt I will ever have to experience again.

In response, we were one of the first countries in the world to shut our borders. We introduced necessary social restrictions to slow transmission. We activated our biosecurity laws and our national pandemic response plan. I brought the leaders of our state and territory governments together to form a national cabinet to ensure our response was as unified and as coordinated as possible within our federated system. In Australia, like in the United States and Canada, our state governments have the constitutional authority for public health, not the federal government. We worked quickly to reinforce our hospital system and secure necessary medical equipment and supplies, including respirators and personal protection equipment (PPE). I even had the army take over a manufacturing plant in Victoria (with the owner's consent) to boost their production of PPE. We introduced a comprehensive testing regimen. We added additional layers of protection around our aged care facilities. We made sure we were able to manufacture our own vaccines. When our vaccine rollout encountered major setbacks in early 2021, I appointed a two-star general to take it over and get it back on track. Day after day we worked the problems we encountered and stood before the public in marathon media conferences to explain our decisions to keep everyone as informed as possible.

We didn't always agree on everything. In the latter stages of the pandemic in 2021, our state jurisdictions took the lockdowns too far, particularly in Victoria. My government also did not support some of the impractical internal border controls on Australia's east coast, although we were wrong to have opposed border closures on the west coast, especially in the courts, during the early stages of the pandemic. But at no stage did my government support vaccine mandates, except in the case of those working with the most vulnerable people in our aged care and health systems. Wider vaccine mandates were imposed unilaterally by some state Labor governments, without the support of my government or the official national medical advice. The federal government had no constitutional powers to override these mandates. We were similarly opposed to the closure of schools by the states, and our opposition to this action was also supported by the national medical advice.

But we can't claim to have gotten everything right. No one in the world did. We had our setbacks and our critics. In a crisis you never get everything right. What matters is how you respond when things don't work out how you planned. However, even with our setbacks, whether it was early on in the rollout of our vaccine program or later when we had trouble obtaining rapid antigen tests, when you look at the results objectively, Australia's pandemic response led the world. Our health plan worked. Compared to the death rates from COVID in other developed countries with comparable health systems, we saved thirty thousand lives. To illustrate, the *New York Times* calculated that nine hundred thousand lives would have been saved in the United States if it had the same death rate as Australia.[2]

When I left office, Australia had the third-lowest death rate from COVID-19 in the developed world.[3] In that first year of the pandemic, before anyone had a vaccine, we restricted the impact of COVID to around 8 percent of our aged care facilities. In the United Kingdom it was seven times greater at 56 percent.[4] When Bill Gates was asked at the Munich Security Conference in 2022 whether it was possible to prevent the next pandemic, he answered, "If every country does what Australia did, then you wouldn't be calling it a pandemic."[5] He called Australia's response to the pandemic the "gold standard."[6] Johns Hopkins University ranked Australia second in the world in pandemic preparedness.[7]

In Australia, we were determined not only to save people's lives but also to protect their mental health. Australians, like all global citizens, were significantly impacted by the fear, anxiety, loss, and isolation they suffered during the pandemic. It was a time of extraordinary uncertainty. Australians were fearful not just for their physical well-being but for their future livelihoods. We were concerned this could be an even worse threat than the pandemic.

The very things that were saving lives during the pandemic and ensuring our hospital system was not being overrun were the same things that would devastate our economy, costing people their jobs, their incomes, their businesses. Once lost, these would take years to restore. Some would never recover. We also understood that lockdowns and other social restrictions would inevitably impact people's mental health. There were no easy calls. We needed to ensure Australians had a country to return to after surviving the pandemic. They would need a job and a business to walk back into. I was particularly mindful of the impact that shutdowns would have on small business owners who had spent their entire lives building up their family businesses. Through no fault of their own, they were about to see it all taken from them instantly as COVID turned off the lights. Such loss would understandably turn people to despair.

I was not prepared to sacrifice one for the other. We had to protect both physical and mental health for the sake of the nation's well-being. We therefore resolved that our pandemic response would be about saving lives *and* livelihoods. As we know all too well, the virus had shut down the world's economy. Planes were grounded, borders closed, businesses shut, supply chains collapsed, and students sent home. If you had asked me a year before if I could have conceived that we would live through such a time, I would have told you it was science fiction. But there we all were. There was no guidebook. Some of the world's largest economies, with the most sophisticated health systems, were collapsing on themselves. We were all staring into the abyss. Once again I would go to my knees in prayer.

As a former treasurer with a background in economics, I knew this would not be like any normal recession or even depression. This would be a synthetic recession. That said, the impacts would be very real and severe. This proved to be the case. To put things in perspective, during the first year of the pandemic, the global economy shrank by more than three percent. That is more than thirty times the magnitude of the economic decline of the Global Financial Crisis of 2009, known in the United States as the Great Recession. This was a major-league economic crisis we had not seen since the Great Depression.

I also knew there was nothing wrong with our economy. Australia was experiencing the longest run of continuous national economic growth of any country in recorded economic history. The danger was letting our economy waste away. We had to make sure we kept our economy as whole as possible, especially as large parts had been forcibly shut down. If we achieved this, then our businesses would be able to snap back when we came out of the pandemic. Along with Treasurer Josh Frydenberg and Finance Minister Mathias Cormann, we got to work and put in place the single largest economic rescue package in Australia's history. Wage subsidies called JobKeeper, income support, business grants, loan repayment relief from the banks, and rent relief from the landlords were just some of the measures we put in place. Thankfully, before the pandemic hit, we had spent the previous six years getting our federal budget back into balance. I spent three of those years as treasurer, knowing that rainy days would always come.

Our economic plan worked. Millions of jobs and hundreds of thousands of businesses were saved. Compared to when the pandemic first struck, Australia's economy grew 4.5 percent by the time we left office in the June quarter of 2022.[8] That's more than South Korea (3.9 percent); the United States (2.7 percent); and the

109

United Kingdom, Canada, and France (all less than 1 percent).[9] The Japanese and German economies were still going backward at that time.[10] Australia's unemployment remarkably fell to the lowest rate in almost half a century.[11] We actually had more jobs after the pandemic than we did before it. Also, despite spending unprecedented amounts on our rescue package, Australia was one of just nine countries to retain our AAA credit rating from all three international rating agencies.[12]

Protecting our economy undoubtedly provided critical relief and peace of mind for millions of Australians, but we knew it would not be enough to prevent the wave of anxiety that would still come crashing over our population. During the pandemic, we saw a massive surge in the need for mental health and counseling services. And we responded. We put in place arguably the largest and most comprehensive mental health response of any country in the world. We poured in the resources and took the advice from our world-leading mental health experts.

My concern for mental health was not new. It had been a long-standing concern. When I was fifteen, my father came into my room and said he needed to tell me something. He looked serious. In chapter 4, I mentioned that my dad was a policeman who ran a youth organization called Boys' Brigade at our local church. Boys' Brigade is a Christian version of the Boy Scouts. Dad had been running the ministry for many years. Mum did the same with Girls' Brigade. Every Thursday and Friday night for forty-five years, except for school holidays, my parents would be at the church hall running their youth programs. They were faithful servants dedicated to helping young people and seeing them come to know Jesus.

On that particular night, Dad came to tell me that one of the older boys who had gone to Brigade had taken his own life. He had leapt to his death from the 56-meter-high (more than 180 feet) sandstone cliffs called "the Gap" near Sydney Heads. He was twenty-two years old. While I did not know Jimmy that well, I knew his brothers. The whole family was involved in the Brigades. Dad knew I would hear about it, and he wanted to tell me directly. I remember being shocked. I had never known anyone who had committed suicide before. I couldn't comprehend it. My world was rocked.

I remember praying to God that night. I prayed for Jimmy's family, but I also prayed for myself. I knew that if it was possible for Jimmy to feel that way, then it was possible for any of us. Jimmy's suicide stayed with me. It constantly reminds me of how hurt people can become in this world and how vulnerable and fragile we are. As time went on I developed a strong interest in mental health. When I was considering becoming a pastor, one of the things that attracted me was the counseling role. It turns out God had other plans for my service.

In politics I was able to follow through on my interest in mental health. As PM it was a thrill to be able to establish and increase funding for mental health programs and services, especially those focused on suicide prevention, eating disorders, and groundbreaking research and treatment for early youth psychosis.

Australia has outstanding and world-leading mental health and counseling services. They are run by highly credible, trusted, and respected nongovernmental agencies. These include Lifeline, Kids Helpline, Headspace, Batyr, and Beyond Blue. During the pandemic, we poured into these resources in record amounts, and it worked beyond what we had hoped. Despite the explosion in demand for mental health services during the pandemic, death by suicide in Australia actually fell. That's right, it fell. The age-standardized rate of deaths per 1,000 people declined by over 7.5 percent in 2020 and 2021 from pre-pandemic 2019 levels.[13] Our prayers were answered.

RUOK?

In 2021, we put a new question in the official census of the Australian population. We asked Australians whether they identified as having a long-term health condition. Of the two in five Australians who said they did, the most prolific condition specified was mental illness.[14] Over two in five adult Australians had experienced a mental disorder at some time in their lives, and one in five had experienced a mental health disorder for at least a year.[15] Of those, anxiety was the most common group of mental disorders.[16] That's around 3.3 million people. In the United States, more than one in five American adults, or nearly 53 million people, experienced a mental health condition in 2020.[17] There is a lot of hurt and anguish going on just below the surface in our communities. Young people are proving to be especially vulnerable. In 2021 the US Surgeon General stated that one in three high school students in the United States, and half of all female students, reported persistent feelings of sadness or hopelessness.[18] Between 2007 and 2018, suicide rates among US youths aged ten to twenty-four increased by 57 percent.[19] In 2020, 629,000 adolescents in the United States attempted suicide.[20]

So how are you feeling? According to the statistics, you may be struggling with anxiety even as you read this. If so, you're not alone.

In Australia we ask, "Are you okay?" We even have a day called RUOK Day. It happens on September 14 each year. It was started by Gavin Larkin. I went to high school with Gav when we were kids growing up in Sydney's eastern suburbs. Gav was in his late twenties and establishing a successful career in advertising when his father, Barry, took his own life. Gav and I had lost contact by then. Thirteen years later Gav started RUOK Day. When interviewed about why he set it up all those years after his father's death, Gav said, "I should have been feeling on top of the world and I felt empty, I felt black, and it really scared me and I started to worry that I might do what my father did."[21]

Gav put his expertise and contacts to work to get RUOK Day off the ground. This included coming to see me in Canberra as I had entered Parliament just a few years before. It was nice to see him. We caught up and reminisced a bit at Aussies café in Parliament House before talking about his new project. I thought it was a terrific idea and encouraged him. The idea is pretty simple: on one day of the year, you simply ask someone, "Are you okay?" It is designed to break down the stigmas and barriers associated with mental illness. To make it okay to talk about it. To make it okay to say you're not okay and talk to someone about it. To put people in touch with the support services they need.

Two years after starting RUOK Day, Gav sadly succumbed to lymphoma at just forty-two. Gav's legacy is quite extraordinary. But he didn't do it for himself. He did it to honor his late father and to ensure others could avoid the suffering his family had experienced. So for Gav's sake, let's talk about it.

Anxiety is different than fear (the subject of the next chapter). When facing imminent danger, a flight response makes sense. I have a fear of heights. Such fears can be very much in the moment. Once the danger passes, so does the fear. The anxiety I'm talking about is not momentary. It lasts much longer and feels inescapable. Such anxiety can be overwhelming.

I had some experience with this as PM and sought help from my doctor in Canberra, who prescribed me with medication that I found very helpful. We are all human. My doctor was amazed I had lasted as long as I had before seeking help. Without this help, serious depression likely would have manifested. It wasn't the difficulty of the pandemic or global challenges I faced in the job that had this impact on me. I would run hard at these challenges every day. In some ways, those challenges kept me sane. What impacted me was the combination of pure physical exhaustion with the unrelenting and callous brutality of politics and media attacks. As a politician, I know this goes with the territory. That's not a complaint or even an accusation. It's just reality. Politicians are not made of stone, yet they're often treated as though they are, including by each other.

Anxiety can be debilitating and agonizing. It doesn't matter if it's rational or not, because how you feel is very real. You dread the future and can't get out of bed. It can leave you feeling hopeless and incapable. It can shut you down mentally and physically. It robs you of your joy and can damage your relationships. I know this from personal experience.

From a clinical perspective, anxiety can also make you sick— headaches, nausea, diarrhea, shortness of breath, and chest pains, just to name a few symptoms. Anxiety can also lead to depression, self-harm, panic attacks, substance abuse, and disrupted sleep patterns. It can affect your appetite and lead to eating disorders. It can even lead to psychosis and other mental illnesses. It requires clinical treatment in its more acute form. Anxiety is not something we can casually dismiss. You can't deal with it by telling yourself to, as we say in Australia, "take a teaspoon of cement and harden up."

It is real, and it can be deadly. We know the majority of people who die by suicide have a mental illness, but this is not always the case.[22] So even if your anxiety has not elevated into a clinical condition, it can still put you at risk. So, once again, RUOK? If you're not feeling okay right now, put down this book, pick up the phone, and call one of the many counseling services that are there to help you. If you're doing okay, then stay with me and let's talk about this a bit more and how I found that prayer and faith can also help.

THE GOD WHO SEES YOU

As prime minister and as treasurer, I met many young people whose lives were being transformed and saved through access to the counseling and other mental health programs we had put in place. I loved these visits. It was one of my greatest joys of being prime minister. One of the things that struck me when I became familiar with how mental health counselors and clinicians engaged their patients was how similar it was to the way God deals with our anxiety and pain. "I see you. I see the pain that you're going through. I can hear you. I'm listening to you. I'm taking you seriously. I'm acknowledging what's happening to you. You are at the center of this conversation. You matter. You are valued."

God knows that anxiety is part of the human condition. He sees you. He knows what you're going through. He knows that it's part of who you are as a human being. There is no shame in it. Anxiety and depression are not a mystery to God.

God was there with Abraham when he walked up the mountain with Isaac to sacrifice him. He was also there for the twenty-five years that Abraham and Sarah waited to have children. He was with Noah on the ark and for the one hundred years it possibly took to build it when people thought he was a crackpot. He was with Joseph in the pit where his brothers had abandoned him and in the prison where he was left to rot. He was with Moses in the wilderness for forty years and with Joshua at the walls of Jericho.

He was with Job through his suffering when Job said, "I am not destroyed by darkness, nor by deep gloom which covers me" (Job 23:17). He was there with David when he was being chased by Saul and despairing for his life. He was with Jonah in the belly of the whale, even though Jonah was running away from God. He was with Shadrach, Meshach, and Abednego as they were led toward the furnace. He was with Daniel in the lions' den and with Nehemiah on the walls of Jerusalem as he was taunted and mocked by his enemies.

He was with Esther as she risked everything and stood before the king on behalf of her people. He was with Ruth as she walked behind the laborers in the field gleaning whatever she could find to feed herself and her mother-in-law. God was with the widow and her son as she prepared to die and made their last meal when Elijah showed up and asked for the first helping. God was with a young teenage girl named Mary when her pregnancy began to show and she was unmarried.

Most of all, God lived among us as a human being. Hebrews 4:15 says, "We do not have a high priest who cannot sympathize with our weaknesses, but One who has been tempted in all things just as we are, yet without sin."

Jesus was not just flesh and blood like us; He can relate to us mentally and emotionally as well. He lived embodied for thirty-three years. He had to deal with the other kids in the village who would have teased him because his mother had gotten pregnant before she was married. He was a teenager experiencing all the feelings you go through as your body changes. He dealt with disappointment and frustration. He dealt with the attacks, lies, cruelty, rejection, and unkindness of others. He suffered betrayal. In the garden of Gethsemane He literally sweated drops of blood in mental agony, vexed by the confrontation between what He knew was God's will for Him and His mortal preference to avoid pain and humiliation.

Jesus not only contended with His own mental challenges; He saw up close and personal what those around Him wrestled with.

He saw how tough it was to be a parent and to make ends meet through his mom and dad. He spent three years traveling around the countryside with twelve anxious young men who had walked away from everything to follow Him. He looked into the wounded heart of Mary Magdalene and saw the pain of a life tortured by abuse and neglect. In the tree he saw the tax collector Zacchaeus, who was despised by his community, and yet He understood his heart. He despaired at the sorrow of the rich young ruler, who had invested all of his self-worth in his possessions and status.

Jesus had an empathy for others like no one who has ever walked the earth. His gaze penetrates to the depths of our souls. In one instant He knows all our pain, all our regrets, all our fears, and all our worries like no one else can.

God wants you to know that He gets it. He's seen it before. He's experienced it before. He knows people who have gone through it before and has walked with them. He understands it. He understands you. He loves you. He knows it's okay to admit you're not okay. He knows we can't do this alone.

He also knows it is important for us to be able to deal with it. In Mark 4:3–12, Jesus told the story of the parable of the sower. Seed is scattered in various places with different outcomes. When talking about the seed that falls among the thorns, Jesus said, "These are the ones who have heard the word, but the worries of the world, . . . choke the word, and it becomes unfruitful" (Mark 4:18–19). He knows that worry will put distance between you and Him. God wants to close that gap. God has acted through Jesus on the cross so that we don't have to worry about who we are, what we've done, and what will happen to us in the future.

Yet we still worry. Thankfully, God has a plan to deal with this as well. Paul set out God's plan in his letter to the Philippians.

STEPS TO PEACE

Philippians 4:6–7 are some of the hardest verses in the Bible to live: "Do not be anxious about anything, but in everything by prayer and pleading with thanksgiving let your requests be made known to God. And the peace of God, which surpasses all comprehension, will guard your hearts and minds in Christ Jesus."

Paul said not to worry about anything. You've got to be kidding me. Nothing to be worried about. Really? What planet was Paul living on?

Before we go too far down that path, let's look a bit closer. Paul was not saying there is nothing to worry about. Of course there is. Paul knew this. Paul was saying we should not respond to the things we worry about with worry. There is a difference.

Worry will not help with the things you are worrying about. Rudolf Abel was right. Jesus said the same thing in Matthew 6:27: "Which of you by worrying can add a single day to his life's span?" There is a better way to deal with the things we worry about than by worrying.

Paul also was not being dismissive of the things we worry about. To the contrary, Paul actually said we've got to do something about them. We can't just ignore them. This will only drive them deeper into our soul. That never ends well. They will find their way to the surface sooner or later, and it won't be pretty. They won't just go away. Satan will make sure of that.

Step one of Paul's plan was to call out the things we worry about. Stop and think about it for a moment. What are you really worried about? Write them down. You will need this list because in step two Paul said you have to raise these things with God Himself. He said, "Let your requests be made known to God." This is where Paul's plan differs from our plan. Under our plan, our worries stay with us. We obsess over things. We lose sleep over them. Under Paul's plan, we transfer ownership of our worries to God. This is not as simple as it sounds. It takes a lot of faith to hand over things like this to God. These are things that are really important to us. If they weren't, we wouldn't worry about them. *What if it doesn't work out the way I want it to? What if God has something different in mind?* These are valid questions. God didn't promise an easy ride. In fact, Jesus said we would share in His sufferings and should rejoice because of it.

Faith has a cost. That cost is control. It requires surrender. Your willingness to do this is a function of whether you really believe that God's plans for you are for your good and not your harm, as it says in Jeremiah. It requires you to trust His plan above your own, above what you feel or what you think you want. Can you really do this? Are you ready for it? Be careful what you wish for before moving to step two. But remember, if you stay at step one, all you will have is a list of worries.

In step two, we set up a meeting with God. At this meeting God wants everything on the agenda. This is not some trial arrangement where you give God some of your lower-order worries, like finding a vacation the whole family can agree on, your next exam, or that presentation coming up at work. It's not a trial run to see how God does with these before moving on to more serious worries like your cancer, your finances, your career, your marriage, and your children. No, God wants it all. If you can't trust God with everything, you cannot trust God with anything.

Step three is to appreciate the nature of the conversation that God wants to have with you at this meeting. Paul said we are to raise everything "in prayer." This means God will really be there. You're not meeting with one of His senior staff. God won't just be dialing in. He will be present with you, and you will have His full attention.

God created prayer as the most powerful way to connect directly with Him. Prayer is intimate. There is no hiding from God in prayer. Through prayer we establish and build a relationship with God.

It brings us closer. Prayer is facilitated by the Holy Spirit, who helps us to say everything we need to say to God. Romans 8:26 says, "The [Holy] Spirit also helps our weakness; for we do not know what to pray for as we should, but the [Holy] Spirit Himself intercedes for us with groanings too deep for words." This is going to be a supernatural conversation, and we will have a supernatural interpreter at our disposal.

Prayer is also a two-way conversation, so expect God to respond. You don't just get to dump your worries at God's door. Expect feedback and get ready to embrace it. That is what we're signing up for when we set this meeting. We'll walk in with our worries and walk out with a set of action items. And there will be regular follow-ups. This is not a one-off meeting. The room has not been booked for just an hour. Prayer doesn't work like that. Prayer is constant. God asks us to pray to Him without ceasing. In 1 Thessalonians 5:17–18, Paul said that ceaseless prayer is the will of God for you in Christ Jesus.

God knows we need to "talk it out" with Him. I love it when my kids talk to me. After I left the job of PM, I had the time to drive my girls to school. Anyone who has parented teenagers knows that one of the best places for real conversations with your teens is when you have their undivided attention. That's how God feels about you. He wants to hear your heart. Daniel understood this, and that is how he prayed to God.

Daniel had a job like a prime minister. I would often turn to the book of Daniel when I was in that job. Daniel was taken from everything he knew in Israel to serve in a place that was hostile to everything about him. Daniel chose to stand firm for God rather than conform to the lifestyle and beliefs of the land he was now living in. Despite this, Daniel regularly found favor with the kings he served. The other officials in the kingdom were constantly jealous of Daniel and plotted against him to bring him down (not a lot has changed in politics).

We read that Daniel prayed three times a day. When attending Parliament or traveling I would always try to speak to Jen at least twice a day and to the girls as regularly as I could. If you care about a relationship, you communicate. Daniel didn't do this out of some religious obligation; he did this because he loved God and could not function without Him. Do you love God and acknowledge that you can't function without Him? I believe the true answer to that question is revealed in how often you pray. You talk to those you love. So when Daniel's enemies in the kingdom conspired to make prayer to God illegal, Daniel didn't skip a beat. He just kept on praying to God as if his life depended on it. Next thing he knew, Daniel was in the lions' den praying once more, and his life depended on it. The rest is history. God delivered Daniel from the lions' den.

What happened to Daniel next is the important bit. Daniel had been studying the prophecies of Jeremiah about Jerusalem and how long it would lay in ruins. Daniel figured out this deadline was approaching. He went to God in prayer and pleading, with fasting, sackcloth, and ashes. He concluded his prayer pleading, "Lord, hear! Lord, forgive! Lord, listen and take action! For Your own sake, my God, do not delay, because Your city and Your people are called by Your name" (Daniel 9:19).

This is the sort of prayer Paul was talking about to the Philippians. Laying our worries at God's feet is not just any prayer. Daniel's prayer was not a one-off. Daniel was in the habit of prayer, establishing communion and trust. You can't just turn this type of prayer off and on. You've got to make prayer and communion a priority in your life if you want to pray the way Paul was saying, in order to be anxious about nothing.

We read that Daniel gave God his full attention. If we expect God to give us His attention, we must give Him ours. Daniel knew he was not a passive partner in his relationship with God. By turning his attention to God, Daniel was demonstrating to Him (and no one else) that this was really important and that he knew that only God could deal with the things he was praying about. Daniel fasted; he wore sackcloth and ashes. Daniel's prayer came with wardrobe, makeup, and a menu (with nothing on it).

In chapter 1, I wrote about having loud conversations with God. I believe this is what Paul talked about when he said to pray with pleading. Being anxious about nothing is not easy. To genuinely hand over our worries to God and be able to trust Him with them and get on with our day is a special type of faith. You have to really want that. There is certainly nothing casual about it. Cry, shout, groan, scream—do whatever comes out of your heart, because you are pleading for God to take this burden of worry away from you and give you the faith you will need to leave it with Him.

In step four we find this meeting will take place in a truly special space. In the Old Testament, before Jesus came to earth, the priests would have to enter the Holy of Holies behind the veil in the temple to commune with God on behalf of the people of Israel. They would have to consecrate themselves before entering. Failure to do so could result in being struck dead. Even at Moses's famous meeting with God at the burning bush, he had to remove his sandals because God told him he was standing on holy ground.

When Jesus died on the cross, the veil that separated the Holy of Holies from the people in the temple was torn from top to bottom.

No more was there any distance. Now we can connect directly with God through prayer. But don't forget, whenever we pray, we have entered a sacred and holy space. In some ways, it is like when I was prime minister and I would go to meet the Queen.

I remember fondly the occasions I met with Her Late Majesty Queen Elizabeth II. For the prime minister of a Commonwealth nation, this was an incredible privilege. The first time was with Jen at Buckingham Palace in July 2019, after our election win. We were both incredibly nervous. In the car on the way from our hotel, Jen was watching a YouTube video of how to curtsy. When we arrived, we got out of the car and were taken through a musty side entrance into a tiny, somewhat ancient elevator. Upstairs we were ushered into a small anteroom. The Queen's longest-serving lady-in-waiting greeted us there and waited with us. Quaint. I couldn't help but notice the small bar heater sitting in front of the fireplace.

We made polite conversation as the Queen's staff ran over the protocol once more. After making our entrance and being greeted by Her Majesty, we would take a seat (after she had sat down, of course). The audience would last about twenty minutes. Her Majesty would then press a button next to her seat and we would be escorted out, being careful not to turn our backs to the Queen. These seemed like very simple tasks, but it was the most nervous I had ever been.

Our meeting with Her Majesty was a delight. Jen nailed the curtsy. After sitting down, I presented Her Majesty with a gift. I had done my homework. Former prime minister John Howard had given me a tip that you couldn't go wrong giving any gift that had something to do with horses. I had the perfect idea: a biography of the famous Australian thoroughbred mare Winx. Winx is the most successful thoroughbred in Australian history, holding the record for the most consecutive wins (thirty-three) and ranked equal first on the Longines World's Best Racehorse rankings. As I presented the gift to Her Majesty, I joked that it wasn't an autobiography and was unsigned, at least by Winx, but if any horse could write and sign an autobiography it would be Winx. She enjoyed the joke, opened the book, and started leafing through the pages, taking a close interest in the photos. She was clearly a fan. I was relieved. Curtsy, check. Gift, check. Now for the conversation.

We spoke about many topics, including events in Australia and the D-Day commemorations we had attended the day before and her own recollections of wartime. She was also interested in our family. Her Majesty took a shine to Jen, and for a while I was a bit of a third wheel in the conversation. Here we were, Jen and Scott from the suburbs of Sydney, having tea with Her Majesty at Buckingham Palace. Somebody pinch me!

We were having a lovely chat. The twenty minutes came and went and we were still there. After almost forty minutes, we finally got up to leave, and Her Majesty took us over to the window to show us where President Trump's helicopter had landed the day before. We also looked at the family photos together on the piano. We then departed, being sure not to turn our backs.

I spoke to Her Majesty again during the pandemic. She never lost sight of the fact that she was Queen not just of England but of the Commonwealth and, in particular, Australia. On my last trip to the United Kingdom, after attending the G7 Summit in Cornwall and meeting with Prime Minister Johnson at Number 10, I met the Queen again in person, this time at Windsor Castle. Once again, Her Majesty was gracious and generous, keenly interested in everything going on in Australia, including the recent mice plague. I was only the second visitor she had received at Windsor after COVID, so she was "up for a chat." President Biden and the First Lady had been there the day before.

What I noticed most about meeting Her Majesty was her ability to be so natural, easygoing, and accessible in her conversation, while at the same time always maintaining her regality. No matter how kind and inviting she was, you never forgot you were speaking to Her Majesty. It offered me a unique, fresh framework for appreciating how our Father God is able to be intimate with us while never surrendering His divinity or majesty. This is an extraordinary combination. We speak to God as an heir through His grace. We speak to Him as a Father. But He is also God Almighty. The space where we meet Him in our prayers is truly sacred. Like Moses, we are standing on holy ground.

In step five, Paul reminds us there must be thanksgiving in our prayers. Daniel understood this also. In his prayer, he acknowledged how God brought His people out of Egypt, and in his prayer, Daniel was asking God to do this all again. Reflecting on God's faithfulness in our own lives not only is a great way to personalize our praises to God, but it also gets our head right. As we recount these in prayer to God, we are reassured of His faithfulness, despite the circumstances we face. For me, thanking God for blessing Jen and me with our two children after fourteen years of waiting (you'll hear more about our infertility journey in chapter 9), reminds me that God can do anything. A spirit of thankfulness boosts our faith. It also gives us hope during suffering.

Finally, after having prayed with pleading and thanksgiving, step six is to expect something to happen. Expect the peace of God that surpasses all understanding to come and guard your hearts and minds in Christ Jesus. As Psalm 94:19 says, "When my anxious thoughts multiply within me, your comfort delights my soul."

We read in chapter 9 that before Daniel had even finished praying, the angel Gabriel turned up and said to Daniel, "I have come now to give you insight with understanding" (verse 22). Wow, that's fast. The moment Daniel started pleading to God in his prayer, God issued His command for action in heaven. That's even faster. God knows what's worrying you. He knows what's burdening you. He knows what you are going to ask Him for. He's waiting for you to engage Him with your whole heart. He wants you to be all in. The second you get into that space, then God is all in. And while you're praying, God is already working.

Jesus taught us to pray, "Your will be done, on earth as it is in heaven" (Matthew 6:10). There is no worry in heaven. That is what God wants for us on earth. You have left your worries with God. You now need to leave them there. They are no longer yours to carry. Let them go. God sends you His inscrutable peace to help you do this. God knows it is hard to let go. Your mind and heart have been doing nothing else but worrying. Imagine the space that is now being created in your heart and mind to pursue the things of God rather than worry. Our intellectual and emotional instincts will try to claw back our worries; that is why God knows that our hearts and minds must be guarded. He is the great "I AM," who was, who is, and who is to come (Revelation 1:8). He's got this. God wants you to have confidence that He's got this. That is why He needs to send His unfathomable peace to calm the sea of your thoughts and emotions.

While you're praying, God is already working.

Before I became PM, before the pandemic, before global anxiety spiked, I visited the outback town of Bourke, in New South Wales. We stopped at a small gallery that had many paintings of outback Australia, but I was drawn to one in particular. It was a striking painting of a ghost gum tree on the bank of the Darling River. In drought this river runs dry. My mind turned to Jeremiah 17:7–8:

Blessed is the man who trusts in the LORD,

And whose trust is the LORD.

For he will be like a tree planted by the water

That extends its roots by a stream,

And does not fear when the heat comes;

But its leaves will be green,

And it will not be anxious in a year of drought,

Nor cease to yield fruit.

When we truly bring our worries to God and leave them with Him, this is just how we will feel. To the extent that I have been able to truly trust God with everything that worries me, I know this to be true. That painting has hung in every office I have had since then—a constant reminder that whatever incredible challenges or terrible anxiety we face, God's peace and His faithfulness will never run dry.

Chapter Seven

WHAT DO YOU FEAR?

"Be strong and courageous! Do not be
terrified nor dismayed, for the LORD your
God is with you wherever you go."
JOSHUA 1:9

Jen and I once visited Queenstown on the South Island of New Zealand for a friend's fiftieth birthday weekend. We had a great time together. Queenstown is the place where bungee jumping was invented. For those who don't know, it involves a 47-meter (141-foot) free fall from a bridge into a deep, narrow gorge with a rushing river below, with a very thick and long "elastic band" tied to your shins and ankles. When you reach the full extension of your leap, you are propelled back vertically toward the bridge at great speed, after which time you bob up and down until coming to a rest. You are then picked up by a life raft waiting in the river below, which takes you to the riverbank. There was no way I was doing this. I am petrified of heights. Jen, however, had also just turned fifty and was feeling adventurous. She decided to take this on and convinced one of our friends to join her in a tandem dive. She was fearless.

Fear is an emotion, like anxiety, but with one key difference. Fear is how we respond to threats that are real and immediate. We get anxious about things that may or may not ever happen. Fear is about something that is about to happen or is actually happening. It sets off a chemical reaction in our brains. The adrenaline shot enables our bodies to fight or take flight from the danger. Many people love the adrenaline shot that comes from this type of feeling. That is why they jump out of airplanes, surf big waves, or bungee jump in Queenstown, like Jen.

When we think of living without fear, we think of being free, uninhibited, decisive, and confident. Brave people know how to overcome their fears. They don't hesitate; they act. By contrast, if we allow it, fear can paralyze, constrict, and silence us. Living in fear attacks our confidence. This is not how we want to live.

The things we fear cannot be avoided. Your appointment with fear is set. It can, unfortunately, show up every day. It could be your cancer diagnosis and treatment, the violence and abuse you are suffering, the poverty you are experiencing, living with the dread of losing a spouse or seeing a relationship fail, or the daily challenges of parenting. It can be the embarrassment of being different or the rejection we feel when we find it hard to make friends. It can be the intimidation of bullies, the relentless attack of enemies seeking to ruin you, or the humiliation of failure. These things are all real, and anyone can be afraid of them, including prime ministers.

God equips us to deal with fear.

In each moment of fear, we choose whether to stand or run. God knows the power of fear to disable, neutralize, and control us. So does Satan. God wants us to stand in the face of these hostile fears, but He knows we cannot do it alone. God equips us to deal with fear. He gave us His Holy Spirit to help us conquer fear, to remain confident of who we are in Him. Isaiah 43:1 says, "Do not fear, for I have redeemed you; I have called you by name." This enabled the apostle Paul to say, "If God is for us, who is against us?" (Romans 8:31), and even if they are, so what?

One day, several years before I became PM, Jen put a small white picture frame on my dresser. It didn't contain a photo of our girls or our family. In the frame was a print of the words God spoke to Joshua after he took over from Moses. It read, "Be strong and courageous! Do not be terrified nor dismayed, for the LORD your God is with you wherever you go" (Joshua 1:9). Jen knew firsthand the daily challenges and demands I faced in politics, and she knew what I needed in order to deal with them. I would look at this and read it every day when I was at home. God gives the same encouragement to everyone He calls to stand for Him, which is all of us. He knows we will need strength and courage.

Through God we can find the strength and courage to call out the lies of fear and to break its power over our lives and the choices we make. Whether we choose to stand in the face of fear is up to us. Thankfully, *how* we are able to stand in the face of fear is up to God.

AN APPOINTMENT WITH FEAR

In the last chapter we talked about Daniel and his experiences in Babylon. He wasn't the only one to face trials and persecution there. He had three really good friends who came with him from Judah. In Australia, we would call them Daniel's mates. Their names were Hananiah, Mishael, and Azariah. They came to Babylon as part of King Nebuchadnezzar's program to take the best and brightest young people from Judah and tutor them to serve in his court. They had to be good-looking, smart, and highly capable. When they arrived, the king gave them new names. Daniel was called Belteshazzar. Hananiah, Mishael, and Azariah became Shadrach, Meshach, and Abednego. They were given the best of everything. Nebuchadnezzar didn't merely want servants; he wanted their loyalty.

Right from the outset, Daniel and his friends chose not to be seduced by what the king was offering. This can be a huge trap in politics and other positions of power. This was yet another area where Jen was a blessing to me. She always kept my feet on the ground. We knew that the trappings of office were temporary. The residences, the vehicles, the travel, the staff—these were not ours; we didn't acquire them. They were attached to the office, not the individuals who held the office. We were just stewards for a time. Jen worked hard to ensure that we kept things modest and preserved what was most important about our home. Our family home has never been about the location. Our values, love, faith, and hospitality make our home strong and hold it together. When Jen invites you to our home, it is personal. When you come to our home, you know you will be treated with dignity and respect. The amazing thing about Jen is, whoever you are, if you are the person in front of her, you are special. This was as true for those who worked at the residences and my personal staff as it was for the many guests at the functions that were held, including ministers, prime ministers, and ambassadors.

Daniel and his mates made the decision to "keep it real" and always remember who they were and where they came from. They were Jews, God's chosen people, and they would honor Him. This meant passing on Nebuchadnezzar's palace buffet and keeping to their Jewish diet. In all other things they were faithful in their training and doing the best they could at their assigned tasks. They did not plan an escape, become activists, or seek to assassinate the king. Like Joseph, they conducted themselves faithfully and trusted God. They performed better than all the others. They were the best in their class, even better than the king's existing and long-standing advisers. Naturally, this created jealousy and resentment.

Long before Daniel found himself in a lions' den, Hananiah, Mishael, and Azariah found themselves at a parade where a massive statue of an idol was being commissioned. Everyone had to bow down. Hananiah, Mishael, and Azariah refused to kneel and remained standing.

There was no avoiding this moment. It could not be wished away. It was going to happen. The choice was straightforward: either kneel and live or stand and die. Nothing they had accomplished would save them from this moment. There would be no special exemptions for being top of the class or having previously found the king's favor. The threat they faced was real, specific, and very present. This was their appointment with fear.

What is interesting is that God didn't rain on the parade. God didn't frustrate the plans of those plotting against them. To the contrary, their enemy's plan worked perfectly. So often we pray for God to remove a situation from us, to put a stop to the attacks. That's okay; we're in good company. King David did this all the time. However, once we've handed this off to God, we have to leave it with Him and press forward. Sometimes we think when the attacks continue that God has forsaken us and that we have somehow failed Him. I can admit to this. I felt this after losing the election. But after many months of prayer and spending time with God after the election, I know it was not true.

God used the painful experience of that loss to draw me closer to Him. He was right there with me. At the end of the year when I lost the election, I was closer to God than I had been at the start. As Paul said in Romans 8:28, God makes all things work together for good for those who are in Christ Jesus.

God wants us to pass through suffering with Him so we are brought into an even closer relationship with Him. Remember, that is why God created us, to have a relationship with Him. That is the point of the gospel of Jesus Christ, for us to have a real, loving, and eternal relationship with God. That is what life, creation, the universe, and eternity are all about. Everything else is subordinate to this from God's perspective.

At the same time, we should also remind ourselves that God has not created the hardships or the suffering. And He certainly doesn't take delight in them. Such hardships are a fact of life when living in a fallen world, corrupted by sin. God will deal with all of this in His final victory (Revelation 21–22), but for now, suffering, fear, and pain are part of life, including losing elections. That is why the Bible talks constantly about suffering. Jesus' life was defined by suffering. Paul said he rejoiced in his sufferings and encouraged others to join him in suffering for the gospel of God (Romans 5:3–5). Peter told us not to be surprised by "fiery ordeals" and that if we are suffering as a Christian, we should not be ashamed but rather glorify God (1 Peter 4:12). So if you're suffering right now, you will find God there. No one knows the territory better than Jesus.

Hananiah, Mishael, and Azariah were dragged before Nebuchadnezzar for refusing to bow to the king's idol. They refused to submit to fear. Nebuchadnezzar gave them a second chance: kneel before my gods, or you are going into the fire. Once again they refused. Nebuchadnezzar was furious. The furnace was intensified. It was so hot that those who took them to the furnace perished because of the heat.

When we read this story, we know it all turns out okay. We know that after the young men were thrown in the fire, a fourth person, whom biblical scholars say was Jesus, was seen walking with them in the fire and that when they came out, their clothes didn't even smell of smoke. But Hananiah, Mishael, and Azariah did not know how things were going to work out. They had to face their fears. They essentially said to Nebuchadnezzar, "If God wants to save us He will, but if He doesn't, well, it's God's call, and that's okay with us. We will not submit to fear and will not bow to your god."

As they were taken toward the fire, no normal human being would have believed anything other than that they were about to be incinerated. That was not a lack of faith in God to deliver them; rather, it was an expression of their incredible faith, demonstrated by their obedience and willingness to leave the outcomes to God. They understood that the ultimate outcome was not going to be played out before this earthly king. They knew that they were part of something eternal, that their God was eternal, and that their relationship with God was eternal.

God is not a vending machine where we insert our faith and expect to receive the comforts of life in return. We don't always get what we want, but we do always get God. That is more than enough. Hananiah, Mishael, and Azariah understood this, so they chose to face their fear with the strength and courage God gave them for that hour.

NO-FEAR POLITICS

One morning in September 2021, I was reading Isaiah 43 where it says, "Do not fear . . . you are Mine . . . I will be with you" (verses 1–2). I sent the following message to my pastor friends: "The events of these past few days and those ahead go beyond our domestic politics. They go to nations, peace, and security. There are great forces at work here, and I have found myself in the middle of them with a great responsibility, and I feel the weight of it. . . . There will be great pressures upon us, as there has been these many years now. I just pray He will walk with me. That I will be humble to His whisper. Please pray; there is so much at stake."

Two days before, I had stood with US president Joe Biden and UK prime minister Boris Johnson to announce AUKUS, a trilateral security pact between Australia, the United Kingdom, and the United States. It was the most significant defense agreement Australia had achieved to protect our national security in seventy years.

There are no three nations in the world that share a greater trust than Australia, the United Kingdom, and the United States. We have the same lens on the world. We hold the same values. We are born of similar traditions. And we fought together on the same battlefields in World War I, World War II, Iraq, and Afghanistan. The AUKUS defense partnership brought these three nations together to equip us with the most advanced and integrated defense technology ever invented to provide a counterbalance to the rising threat of an increasingly assertive and authoritarian Communist Chinese regime threatening the stability of the Indo-Pacific region. The centerpiece of the agreement was for Australia to acquire nuclear-powered, conventionally armed submarines. The United States had shared this technology only once before with another country—the United Kingdom, in 1958. Previous Australian governments had tried and failed to be granted access, as had other American allies. This was the holy grail we needed to provide for Australia's security in the Indo-Pacific.

Over a year before, in July 2020, I had updated Australia's national defense strategy.[1] I warned we were witnessing the same dangerous combination of destabilizing forces in the Indo-Pacific that we had seen with the Japanese in the 1930s. Those forces led to the bombing of Pearl Harbor during World War II. I believed we could avoid history repeating itself if we heeded the lessons of that time. This meant not being complacent or blind to the threat. Nor could we continue to indulge in passive appeasement of China's assertiveness. We could not give in to fear. Such appeasement would only serve as an invitation. During the Obama administration, China had surged into the South China Sea, turning island atolls into airports. China was testing the West, pushing as far as they could. No one said no. Those atolls are now military installations resembling stationary aircraft carriers that threaten our region.

The AUKUS agreement, and the acquisition of nuclear-powered submarines and other cutting-edge defense technology, was key to our plan to resist Chinese coercion and ensure an enduring strategic balance that supported peace and stability in our region. To understand what we were up against, let me share a bit more of the backstory on China and Xi Jinping that led to AUKUS.

Xi Jinping became the general secretary of the Communist Party of the People's Republic of China (PRC) at the 18th People's Congress in 2012. Xi's appointment was a turning point for China and the world. At the time, the prevailing view was that Xi would further modernize and grow China's economy while conducting important domestic reforms, including dealing with entrenched corruption. There was also hope for increased international engagement, including cooperation on global issues like climate change and maybe even human rights and religious freedoms. Xi came across as a savvy, modern, and internationally engaged political leader with a positive agenda, a notch above his predecessors.

I first met President Xi when he addressed Australia's national parliament in November 2014.[2] It was his sixth visit to Australia and his first as president. He hit all the right notes. He spoke admiringly of our koalas and flattered us for our friendliness and our ingenuity, noting that Australian scientists had invented Wi-Fi. He quoted wise Chinese proverbs and celebrated our economic partnership. He also spoke of his ambitions for China. He told us he intended to realize "the Chinese dream" through opening up, promoting the rule of law, and driving modernization. It was a full charm offensive. Xi's message was clear: there was nothing to fear from a rising and stronger China in our region.

This was a message the world had been wanting to believe about China since at least the Clinton administration in the early nineties. A growing Chinese economy was good for the world economy. Everyone would benefit. Furthermore, a more affluent China, with an expanding middle class, would ultimately lead to a more liberalized and possibly even democratic China. Or so we thought. This proved to be, arguably, the most misplaced assumption in international relations since Neville Chamberlain proclaimed "peace in our time" upon his return from Munich in 1938.

The reality has proven to be very different. Xi's real ambition is a neo-Marxist mission to overturn what he refers to as China's "century of humiliation" at the hands of "Western imperialism." He seeks to achieve this by realizing China's destiny of hegemonic power in the Indo-Pacific, reunifying Taiwan with China (by force if necessary), centralizing and asserting Beijing's authority at home (resulting in human rights abuses in Xinjiang and Hong Kong), and rewriting the rules of the global order in China's favor.

To back up these plans, President Xi said he wanted a Chinese military (the People's Liberation Army, or PLA) that was able to win wars.[3] There are no prizes for guessing who these wars would be against. As PM, I received regular briefings on the status and projection of China's military power and buildup. While I cannot share those details, the annual report published by the US Department of Defense to Congress on China provides a clear enough picture.[4] At the time of writing, the PLA is already one of the largest militaries in the world with around 2.2 million service members on active duty.[5] China also has, numerically, the largest navy in the world with a battle force of 340 ships and submarines, including twelve domestically built nuclear submarines and more on the way.[6] In 2024, China's second domestically built aircraft carrier will be commissioned for service.[7] China is also improving its capability to counter submarine activity in the region through its surface ships and aircraft.[8]

This was significant to Australia, as we were in the early planning stages of acquiring twelve conventional diesel-powered submarines from France. The advance in China's anti-submarine capabilities meant that conventional submarines, like the ones we would be building, would be far more restricted in the future. Diesel subs have to come up for air; it's called "snorting." When they do this, they are spotted. The whole point of a submarine is to operate undetected for long periods of time. This is what nuclear-powered submarines can do, and they can travel long distances. It was now likely our new conventional submarines would be obsolete before they even got wet.

China also has the largest air fleet in the region and the third largest in the world, with around 2,250 combat aircraft including fighters and bombers.[9] By the end of 2022, China had 400 operational nuclear warheads and is likely to have 1,500 by 2035.[10] This is backed up by a growing arsenal of intercontinental ballistic missiles with a range of 5,500 km (3,400 miles), potentially able to reach the Australian mainland, and the world's leading technology in hypersonic missiles.[11]

Together with Russia and Iran, the PRC also leads the world in state-sponsored cyberattacks. We experienced them regularly in Australia during my time in government. The first shots fired in any war will not be bullets but rather bits and bytes disabling military systems and civil infrastructure.

As you can see, China is working hard to make sure it can back up its threats.

NO DEAL

When I visited President Trump at the White House in 2019, I told the crowd gathered on the South Lawn that when it comes to Australia's national security, we may look to the United States, but we will never leave it to the United States, and I meant it. We are a proud nation that carries our own water. The United States would be vital to helping us deal with the threats we were facing in our own region, as they always have been, but we had to do our part as well. When our party came to government in 2013, we promised to restore our annual investment in our defense forces from the lowest levels in more than seventy years to 2 percent of gross domestic product (GDP, the size of our national economy). We achieved and exceeded this while I was PM.

Many in Australian politics, the media, and the business community wanted Australia to keep our head down about China. "Why do we have to call China out?" they would say to me. China was our largest trading partner. Why do we have to lead the offensive? Why can't we leave it to someone else? My answer was always, "If not Australia, then who?" Unlike most other Western countries, Australia lives in the Indo-Pacific and is surrounded by developing and smaller countries already vulnerable to China's coercion or already compromised by their influence. We had the most to lose if things stayed on their current course. Someone had to say no. I decided it would be me.

I decided it was not in Australia's long-term interests to duck and cover. We had to stand up for ourselves, face our fears, and not capitulate to China's bullying. This meant we had to be prepared for the reprisals that would come our way and be ready to tough them out when we took action. This would include causing some discomfort in our own region, where most countries in Southeast Asia would prefer not to rock the boat when it comes to dealing with China. I understood those countries could certainly not afford to antagonize China and would not be able to publicly support us when taking such action. I knew they may even be critical, but I also knew they would be key beneficiaries in terms of their own sovereignty. Thankfully, the Australian public was strongly in agreement with the stand we would take.

As treasurer, I had already said no to Chinese investors buying Australia's largest cattle station. The Chinese government was deeply offended. They were also offended when I said no to them gaining strategic interests in our energy, telecommunications, and data infrastructure. We further strengthened our foreign investment policies to protect Australia's interests. This included gaining authority to say no when our state and territory governments unilaterally sought to sell strategic assets to foreigners, including China, after our provincial government in the Northern Territory unilaterally leased the Port of Darwin to a Chinese-owned company, which the federal government at that time had no authority to prevent and certainly did not approve.

Our resistance also extended to denying Chinese companies any role in building our 5G telecommunications network. With 5G and the Internet of Things (IOT), you can potentially switch household appliances on and off, as well as electric vehicles, power systems, mobile phone networks, and much more. My predecessor, Malcolm Turnbull, bravely created new laws to prevent Chinese interference in our universities and political system, and we supported our Southeast Asian neighbors when they pushed back against China's incursions and claims in the South China Sea. But it was my call for an independent inquiry into the origins of COVID that angered the Chinese government the most. How dare we? COVID-19 had killed millions of people and shut down the global economy, and Australia had the audacity to want to know how it started in order to prevent this kind of catastrophe from happening again. I will never regret that call.

The Chinese government responded by imposing illegal trade restrictions on Australian products and putting Australia in the diplomatic deep freeze, engaging in regular public tirades against Australia. There were no more speeches about our lovely koalas and how we had invented Wi-Fi. The Chinese government was trying to coerce us into submission. They did not expect our response. They seemed confused by it. Why couldn't Australia just go along with the same deal everyone else was taking? *You can keep getting rich off China so long as you agree not to get in our way or question what we are doing in the region, whether in China, another country, or your own.*

Many countries have taken this deal with China, including many Western and European countries. Some shamelessly seek it, beating a path to Beijing. I was happy to trade with China, but our values and sovereignty were not up for sale. I refused to allow China to intimidate us and have our nation live in fear. Instead, we set about building our resilience, strengthening our defenses, diversifying our economy and trading relationships, and working even more closely with our like-minded friends, especially the United States, Japan, India, and the United Kingdom. Our actions inspired others to do likewise. This is where AUKUS came in.

PROJECT FREEDOM

In late 2018, not long after becoming PM, I became concerned that our French submarine project was falling behind schedule. I was given assurances the project would be kept on track, including by President Emmanuel Macron of France. I resolved privately to revisit this again after the election. The following year things worsened. On the night we won the 2019 federal election, I received a congratulatory text message from President Macron, inviting me and Jen to visit Biarritz in a few months' time to attend the G7. Emmanuel had picked up that I was concerned about the project. I recall remarking once to him that the project was becoming friendless in Australia. He acknowledged the problems and had taken steps to remedy them. Still, this was becoming a major issue. It was at this point that I began to realize we may need a plan B.

Usually a plan B means settling for a worse option. But, I wondered, what if we could come up with a better one? What if we could get what we had always needed—access to nuclear-powered submarines? The strategic environment in the Indo-Pacific was changing rapidly. Our risk was increasing. Nuclear-powered submarines had gone from a nice-to-have to a need-to-have. I realized this would be our last chance for Australia to ever acquire a nuclear submarine capability. I was not going to leave office one day and wonder about what could have been.

I discussed it with my chief of staff, Dr. John Kunkel, and called my senior defense adviser, Jimmy Kiploks, into my office and shut the door. I asked Jimmy, "Do you think nuclear-powered subs are even possible?"

Jimmy is the type who doesn't say much. He knows his stuff and gives straight answers. "Yeah, I reckon," he said.

I asked him to have some discreet discussions with key people in the Defense Department over the summer break and come back to me. A few weeks later in the new year, Jimmy quietly walked back into my office in Canberra and said, "Yeah, they reckon it's worth a go." So we began.

Over the next year, as COVID-19 ravaged the world, a small project team in the Defense Department in Canberra went to work finding out what it would take to convince the United States to let us access their technology to build and operate nuclear-powered submarines. At that time, we were only looking at the next-generation British *Astute*-class submarine known as the SSN-R. The Americans had not yet indicated an interest in one of their designs being considered, such as their *Virginia* class. A year later we got our answer. Key figures in the US naval establishment and those responsible for stewardship of the nuclear submarine technology would not stand in the way of considering our proposal. This still did not mean a yes, but we could now confidently elevate the discussion to a political level.

In late June 2021, on a clear summer evening, President Biden, Prime Minister Johnson, and I met at the G7 in a small room overlooking a tranquil Carbis Bay in Cornwall. While the view was spectacular, the modesty of the room jarred with the magnitude of the issues we were discussing. For something like this, you might expect oil portraits with gilded frames on oak-paneled walls, with large chandeliers hanging above a long, thick majestic oak table. Instead, three dining chairs were pulled from the restaurant next door and positioned in the corner of the room, with some flags hastily placed behind each of our seats.

I was confident. I had prepared exhaustively for the meeting, going over my pitch numerous times. Prior to the meeting, key national security advisers from each country had been meeting for weeks and were keen to get a result at this meeting to head off any risk that the project might leak to the media. This was a big deal. I knew that the president would have to be comfortable with the decision. And this was only our first discussion of the proposal at this level.

The president was favorably disposed but still had some questions and a few issues he wanted to spend some more time on, in particular the ramifications for nonproliferation. That was fine with Boris and me. Boris and I had been directly discussing AUKUS since May. He used to call it Project Freedom. We agreed on a "where to go from here" plan and hoped to conclude the agreement in late July. It would end up taking longer than that. These things always do. The process from here would also now include considering a US boat, which ended up being part of the final plan announced by my successor. We were close, but we were not there yet. It could still all fall down. I still needed option A.

We went outside after the meeting, and I walked down the stairs with Boris and Joe. All the other leaders were gathered outside getting ready for one of those grinning photos you see of leaders on the TV news at these events. After the photo, President Macron approached me. We walked together down the stairs to the beach-front for an informal dinner reception. This was not the time for a conversation about submarines, so we just exchanged pleasantries and small talk. We had arranged to have dinner at the Élysée Palace in Paris on my way home from the United Kingdom the following week. It would just be the two of us. I would wait until then.

STRATEGIC MOVE

I rolled up to the large courtyard of the almost three-hundred-year-old presidential palace, Élysée, that had accommodated French presidents since Napoleon's grandson in 1848. I was greeted warmly by President Macron, and we held a brief media conference before entering the palace. He walked me to the back patio where our table overlooked the palace's immaculate gardens. Suffice it to say, I was impressed and quite overwhelmed. Once again, a boy from the beachside suburbs of Sydney was a long way from home. There we were in Paris, on a ridiculously pleasant summer evening, about to sit down to probably one of the finest meals I'd ever had. I assure you, my preference was to just relax and enjoy the evening. But that wasn't on the agenda.

Up until then, my relationship with President Macron had been positive and friendly. He was smart and charming, and we shared a passionate interest in the Pacific Island nations. As a prime minister, though, you cannot allow the sentimentality of your relationships to take precedence over your national interest. We exchanged gifts and some friendly conversation, but I knew I would have to turn the subject to submarines. Even though AUKUS had not yet landed, I could not leave that dinner without making it clear we were reconsidering our position on Australia's submarine project with France.

I made it clear that this was not about missed deadlines or the project difficulties we had experienced thus far in the partnership. If we proceeded with the French submarines, I was confident those issues could be ironed out, but I also knew it would mean further delays and that it would not be until 2038 that we would see the first submarine. It was also not about any deficiency in the French design. The French submarines were still the right choice if we were looking for a conventionally powered submarine. That was just no longer what Australia needed, and I made this clear.

I also explained that there had been significant changes in the strategic environment in the Indo-Pacific. We discussed these changes and their implications. I said this meant conventionally powered submarines would no longer do the job we needed them to do. We needed nuclear-powered submarines. I told the president we were going to have to look at other options.

President Macron naturally wanted to know what these other options were. I said I couldn't discuss those with him at this stage. I explained that we had not made a final decision, which we had not. Option A could still turn out to be our only option, and I had to keep it alive. Emmanuel asked to send his senior defense people to Australia to sit down with ours to talk the issue through. I agreed but said we would have to do it quickly. Emmanuel said to me, "I don't like to lose."

I had expected that our discussion of the submarine contract would bring our evening to a quick end. Generously, this didn't occur. Emmanuel was a gracious French host. We continued to chat for about another hour before he kindly gave me a tour of the palace, even showing me some original documents signed by Napoleon himself. Quite amazing. We said goodbye on the palace steps, and I went back to our hotel and debriefed my senior national security team.

The next day the French defense establishment went into overdrive, contacting every Australian official they could. Soon after, my ministers for defense and foreign affairs were also contacted by their French counterparts. It was clear that President Macron had sent a rocket into his government and was pressuring his defense officials to get the project fixed. These actions signaled that he knew the contract was under threat. The next morning I had breakfast with my friend and former finance minister, Mathias Cormann. Earlier in the year, in one of Australia's most successful diplomatic campaigns, we had secured the election of Mathias as our nominee for the position of secretary-general to the OECD (the Organization for Economic Cooperation and Development). He had just taken up the post and was living in Paris. After breakfast, I addressed the thirty-four OECD member country ambassadors from the world's most advanced developed economies and held a media conference in the OECD foyer. At the media conference I was predictably asked about the French submarine contract. I confirmed I had discussed the issue with President Macron and purposefully noted that contracts have "gates" in them for a reason. I noted we were still yet to pass through the critical gate that the French contractor, the Naval Group, which is owned by the French government, had missed the previous December. Phil Coorey is an experienced and respected journalist in the Canberra Parliamentary Press Gallery. He used to refer to my media approach as dropping breadcrumbs for the media to follow. On this occasion Phil would have called this "a whole loaf." Still, no one really picked up on it. Phil wasn't in Paris that day.

After returning from Europe we continued working with the United States and the United Kingdom to finalize our agreement. I wrote to President Macron reinforcing the points I had made at our dinner discussion. The French sent Vice Admiral Bernard-Antoine Morio de L'Isle to Australia to sort things out. Our defense team met with him and set out our assessments and reasoning, as I had done in Paris. The admiral did not agree with our assessment of the strategic situation in the Indo-Pacific nor the implications it had for our submarine program. This highlighted the problem. France wanted their contract and would not see past their own commercial interests. We wanted the best submarines to protect our national security. Our goals no longer aligned.

I have always assumed the French government and President Macron thought I was bluffing and just trying to squeeze them on the deal. They probably never believed that we could have pulled off something like AUKUS. I was not bluffing. I never bluff. The French failed to appreciate just how seriously we were taking the threat to our security in the Indo-Pacific.

As each week dragged on, it became harder and harder to maintain security over the project. More and more people became aware across the US, UK, and Australian systems as we worked to finalize the AUKUS arrangement. We also knew we would have to give France formal notification of our decision not to proceed. If the French were given enough opportunity, I knew they would knock AUKUS over. They would deploy their considerable diplomatic resources to kill the AUKUS deal to protect their contract. I needed to wait until I had a firm date for the announcement. You don't jump off one lily pad unless you have another one to land on. I could not risk it all unraveling.

The day before the announcement, I sent a message to President Macron, letting him know I had been endeavoring to schedule a call with him for a few days. He was proving elusive. He came back to me personally with a time that would have been too late. He asked in his text message, "Should I expect good or bad news for our joint submarines ambitions?" This was not a question from someone who was oblivious to our concerns or the mortality of his submarine contract. He had not been misled as was later claimed. I suppose admitting that the French government had failed to take what we were saying seriously, or that there had been a complete failure of their intelligence services, would have been more embarrassing. I replied saying we needed to speak that day. In the absence of any response, later that night in Canberra (by then morning in Paris) I sent a letter directly to President Macron via secure direct message advising him that we were ending our submarine contract and proceeding to acquire a nuclear submarine capability with the Americans and the British. The next morning, Australian time, I would be standing up with President Biden and Prime Minister

Johnson to launch AUKUS. It was the longest night of my prime ministership. The French had almost twelve hours to topple the deal. Thankfully, they were unable to do so. Our patience and preparations had paid off.

In response, France recalled its ambassador, the French president publicly called me a liar and called into question Australia's capability to undertake the new project, and French diplomats did everything they could to sabotage the arrangement. I had read them correctly. There was also some discomfort from some of our Southeast Asian partners in Indonesia and Malaysia about the secrecy surrounding the arrangement and not having been consulted in advance. Of course they would have preferred to have known more about it before it was announced. Ideally, we would have liked this also. However, such an approach would have made AUKUS impossible to achieve. My critics said we could have also avoided offending France if we had given them formal notification earlier. This was naive, as such notification would have only been used by France to disrupt the deal with the United States and the United Kingdom and make sure AUKUS never happened. There is no way to end a $90 billion contract where the other party walks away happy. But it had to be done.

I am pleased the new government in Australia is once again speaking with France and is also able to now engage more proactively with our neighbors in the region about AUKUS, but that is their luxury. Were it not for our courage to take the actions we did at the time and our preparation to suffer short-term discomfort and even personal reputation damage, AUKUS never would have happened. There is a reason Australia had not achieved anything on this scale for seventy years. Such achievements come at a cost, and those who wish to pioneer such advances must be prepared to accept that cost. I was.

My foreign minister, Marise Payne, had rightly warned from the start that AUKUS would damage our relationship with France. That was inevitable. And I accepted it. That is why it was such a hard decision. I had to choose between ensuring Australia was better able to protect itself for generations to come from the most significant threat we had faced since we were bombed by Japan during World War II, or facing the fury of an offended French president. I chose to stand up to those seeking to bully us and put up with the storm from the French. The alternative was to let fear control my decisions and do nothing, leaving Australia exposed and weakened.

Facing your fears means taking risks and contending with difficult choices. There are always costs. There will be discomfort, uncertainty, and oftentimes great loss. That promise from God that He would always be with me, which Jen had framed and put on my dresser, meant that when the time came I knew I could be "strong and courageous" and did not have to be "terrified nor dismayed." That doesn't mean there are no consequences for the choices we make or that we always get it right. Nor does it mean that God is telling us what to do. It just means that whatever the outcome, God is there with us, and we don't have to fear or be intimidated. Hananiah, Mishael, and Azariah understood there would be life-and-death consequences when they said no to Nebuchadnezzar. They also knew that wherever they went, including a furnace, God would be with them, and He was. I knew the same.

I wasn't reckless in the decisions I took to stand against China's bullying or to cancel the French submarine contract. I carefully weighed those decisions. The threats to Australia, which we continue to face, are very real. However, my decisions were not made from a mindset of fear. When we let fear make our choices, we are serving those who are the source of our fear; we are letting them command us and control our decisions. That is why they intimidate;

that is why they bully. God's assurance enabled me to step out of a mindset of fear and do what I believed was in the best interest of my country. God was the source of my strength and courage.

THE FEAR OF GOD

Okay, just one final thought: If God doesn't want us to live in fear, why do we read in the Bible that we should fear Him? In Deuteronomy 10:12–13, God told Israel, "What does the LORD your God require of you, but to fear the LORD your God, to walk in all His ways and love Him, and to serve the LORD your God with all your heart and with all your soul, and to keep the LORD's commandments and His statutes which I am commanding you today for your good?" Isaiah 33:6 says the fear of the Lord should be our treasure.

King Solomon, the wisest man ever to have lived, said in Proverbs that the fear of God is "the beginning of wisdom" (9:10). He said that the fear of the Lord is to hate evil, pride, arrogance, the evil way, and the perverted mouth. In Acts 9:31, Luke cited the fear of the Lord as the reason the church in Judea, Galilee, and Samaria enjoyed peace and was being built up. Even Jesus feared the Lord and delighted in it, according to Isaiah 11:2.

I have always found it jarring to use the word *fear* when talking about our relationship with God. I understand the theological explanation. The scholars (I am not one) say that the references to fear in these passages speak of a reverence and respect for God and who He is. In one of the many Tim Keller sermons I have listened to, Tim describes the fear of God as the joyful, humbling awe and wonder we feel before the salvation of God. He says, "On the one hand it affirms you to the sky, but at the same time it humbles you into the dust."[12] Fair enough, but it is also true that the Hebrew and Greek words used for fear in these passages, whether they are encouraging us not to fear our adversaries or to fear God, are the same. Again, the scholars will tell us that context is important. But it still bothers me. Why do I have to fear someone whom I love and who says they love me? I know that I must show reverence and respect, but why does the Bible describe this as fear?

In this chapter, we have talked about how fear can try to control us. It is a powerful emotion. It can direct our choices. It is based on things that are very real. What I think God is saying is that fear itself is not the issue. Fear is just a natural emotional response. The issue is not fear; it is about the control that will be exercised over you if you surrender to that fear. When faced with those who seek to intimidate, control, and harm you, God says we should not fear. This includes circumstances as much as people. But fear of a benevolent majesty, whose plans and purposes are for our good, is something very different. For such a one as this we can submit, in reverence and awe.

Isaiah 8:12 says, "You are not to fear what they fear or be in dread of it." God does not want our lives to be controlled by the things the world wants us to fear. God wants to liberate us from that. Instead we are reminded in verse 13, "It is the LORD of armies whom you are to regard as holy. And He shall be your fear. And He shall be your dread." It's a strange choice of language but deliberate. God knows that our fear and dread can totally control us. So He is saying let Him be that: "I am the One who is Holy." God says, "You can follow Me. Let Me be what guides your life, not the things you dread, that seek to harm you and do not have your best interests at heart. They just want to control, manipulate, and intimidate you." When you truly change what you are afraid of in life, "then [God] will become a sanctuary" (verse 14). What safer place is there than that? The good news is that God's sanctuary is like an RV; it travels with you. God promises, "When you pass through the waters, I will be with you; and through the rivers, they will not overflow you. When you walk through the fire, you will not be scorched, nor will the flame burn you. For I am the LORD your God . . . your Savior" (Isaiah 43:2–3).

Chapter Eight

WHO ARE YOU FOLLOWING?

"Do not be afraid, for those who are with us are greater."
2 KINGS 6:16

I like to watch Marvel movies with my girls. *Guardians of the Galaxy* is my favorite (I'm a big fan of Rocket). I started watching them with my girls when I was PM as a fun thing to do together. According to my loving daughters, I can be really annoying when I watch Marvel movies. I apparently ask too many questions. "So what is her special power again?" or "So who's that guy again?" I'll ask mid-scene. Abbey just rolls her eyes and then tries to explain to her Gen X dad the complexities of the multiverse. Lily just laughs.

When I was growing up, my favorite superhero was Batman. He was quite different than today's CGI version. There were no perfect abs, self-fitting armor, or complex backstories. In the 1970s, my Batman wore purple tights and black underwear over the top. Together with Robin, Batman could effortlessly walk up the walls of buildings holding on to only a thin Bat Rope. They would then burst through a tenth-floor window, catching the Riddler, or some other villain, and all their goons by surprise. An overly choreographed fight scene would ensue—*Kapow! Wham! Smack!*—and it would all be over. See you next week.

Batman's urban mountaineering abilities so inspired me as a kid that one weekend when I was about nine I decided to give this wall-climbing caper a go. If Robin had been there, I would have heard, "Holy stupidity, Batman!" I found some rope and a wall and put my Bat skills to the test. While I didn't end up in the hospital, it certainly didn't end well. After some rope burns, cuts, bruises, and grazes, I gave up trying to walk up walls. I knew I would never be Batman (sigh). The secret to Batman's wall-climbing abilities had eluded me. Just how did he do it? Perhaps it was those special tights? It was my older brother, Alan, who unraveled the mystery of camera rotation for me. "You're telling me it's not real?!" I exclaimed. I was a constant amusement to my older brother when I was growing up, including on another weekend when I thought I could be Spiderman and jumped off a roof. Again, it didn't end well, but once again I managed to cheat the local hospital emergency room.

My parents used to tell these stories from time to time at my expense. My children now know them. Dad would just laugh. Mum would try to redeem something in her telling to encourage me. She would say, "He was just a very determined young boy." Again, how good are mums!

There's nothing wrong with having heroes who inspire and guide us. While wall climbing may not have been Batman's best example for me to follow, as societies we have told morality tales for millennia to educate our children and teach them important values and life lessons. These tales can be fictional, real, or a combination of both. Learning from others' experiences is what makes us who we are. Our lives and values are the sum of the many narratives and influences we have been exposed to, positive and negative.

HEROES IN THE REAL WORLD

Throughout my life I have consumed my fair share of political biographies. I continue to read them. I underline them. I write comments in the margins. I often refer back to them. Of all the political lives I have studied through various biographies, the most influential and my most admired are Teddy Roosevelt (TR) and Australia's tenth prime minister, Joseph (Joe) Lyons, who led Australia out of the Great Depression.

Both of these leaders knew what they believed and what they had to do. They weren't trying to prove anything to anyone. They also did not try to fit neatly into the partisan or ideological boxes others defined for them. As a result, both were somewhat orphaned by their own partisan movements after their time in office. Both found themselves in power through unexpected circumstances or an unexpected chain of events. They had to deal with the events as they found them, not as they had hoped for. "For such a time," perhaps, as God said of Esther (Esther 4:14). This all has a familiar ring to me.

TR is well known, but let me tell you a bit more about Joe Lyons, drawing from Anne Henderson's great biography.[1] Joe was a schoolteacher from northern Tasmania, Australia's only island state, south of the mainland. His passion for education drew him initially to the Labor Party and state politics, where he became a successful and pragmatic state premier. Joe and his wife, Enid, were also committed Catholics. After Enid's first two miscarriages, doctors said she would never have children. They would go on to have twelve children, tragically losing one of them in infancy and one in another miscarriage. Joe entered federal politics in 1929. Two days after the election, the stock market on Wall Street collapsed. Within a year Joe Lyons was put in charge of the Treasury. In this role Joe refused to engage in the ideology and politics of the Depression and went looking for practical solutions. Lyons worked closely with state governments, the central bank, and creditors to pull together a plan.

Many in his own Labor Party opposed his policies and were calling on him to default on our national debt and engage in massive public-spending programs. Lyons resisted. He understood that at that time Australia's future depended heavily on being able to raise capital, especially from British banks, both during and after the economic crisis. This meant he had to follow a more orthodox economic path to secure the support of Australia's creditors. This meant getting government budgets under control, not unleashing spending that the nation could not finance. Had Lyons embraced the path being urged by most in the Labor Party at the time, Australia's economy would have gone down the Argentinian road and suffered the fate of the many failed economies of Central and South America. Instead, Australia emerged from the Depression, along with Great Britain, sooner and stronger than most other developed nations, including the United States, just as we have more recently done from the COVID recession.

Joe Lyons ended up resigning from the Labor government and setting up a new conservative political party, which became the forerunner to my own party, the Liberal Party. He went on to win the next three federal elections.

Joe Lyons's practical focus on what was needed in Australia (rather than mimicking the responses of other nations, indulging ideology, or chasing political populism) would be an important guide to me when our government confronted the COVID-19 pandemic and the recession it caused. As with Lyons back in the 1930s, we would have to make our own Australian way to ride through the crisis successfully.

As a leader, you don't get to choose the circumstances in which you govern. You can have all the grand visions and ambitions for government you like, but events will quickly cure you of that vanity. Your first job is to deal with what is right in front of you, and then you do whatever you can to strengthen the country so those who follow you can contend with their challenges more effectively. I have learned from TR and Joe Lyons, and many others I have studied, that true legacies are built not by leaders who are obsessed with their place in history but by those who know what they are about, get on with the job in front of them, and put the national interest first. Let history write itself. When you know your story is already written in the Book of Life, what is written in other books takes on much less significance.

LEARNING FROM LIVING MENTORS

Even better than studying the leaders of history is learning from living mentors. You are unlikely to be the first person to deal with a situation. The best mentors understand that they are not there to tell you what to do or even to approve of what you are doing. They understand that you are not their proxy. They know they are there to help you develop your potential. The best mentors help you organize your thoughts, challenge your thinking, and help you find your own way forward.

During the pandemic I would regularly speak to former prime minister John Howard. When I was treasurer, I would often talk to former treasurer Peter Costello. John's early and most important advice to me and my treasurer, Josh Frydenberg, at the start of the pandemic was that there is no place for ideology in a crisis. You just do what you have to do and let the commentators and critics say whatever they like.

I also found a mentor in the former prime minister of Japan, the late Shinzo Abe. Shinzo was the most impressive and insightful leader I met during my time as prime minister. We first met under the blazing sun in Darwin in late 2018 when he made a special visit to Australia to lay a wreath at our war memorial commemorating the victims of the numerous bombing raids on Darwin by the Imperial Japanese Army during the Pacific War. I greeted Shinzo and his wife, Akie, on the curbside, and we walked together in silence across the lawn in front of the memorial, holding our floral tributes. We placed them quietly together on the memorial. There were no speeches. There was no pageantry, just a quiet and humble act of grace. After paying our respects, Shinzo walked over to meet and speak with the families of veterans who were gathered in the shade under a nearby marquee.

This simple ceremony was arguably the most significant event I attended during my term as PM. Here I was, the grandson of Gunner Leslie Smith, who fought against the Japanese in Papua New Guinea and Borneo as part of Australia's 2nd/5th Field Regiment, standing side by side with a Japanese prime minister seeking to put to rest the ghosts of the terrible violence of that war, more than seventy years later. The visit was Shinzo's initiative. He had performed the same ceremony at Pearl Harbor. It was a genuine act of healing.

Later that day we sat down for our first one-on-one discussion and formal bilateral conference. High on the agenda was a proposed agreement that would allow our respective defense forces to train and operate in each other's territory. It would be the first such agreement that Japan had entered into with any other country in the world. The agreement had been stalled for several years. It would take me another three years to get the deal done. At a private dinner that night, Shinzo and I discussed the future of the Indo-Pacific and the pressures we collectively faced from an increasingly assertive China. Shinzo had been dealing with these issues for many years. Apart from his grace and humility, Shinzo also possessed the qualities Jesus spoke of when sending His disciples out among "wolves" as He exhorted them to be "as wary as serpents" and "as innocent as doves" (Matthew 10:16). This summed up Shinzo Abe pretty well.

I listened carefully. Shinzo was an extraordinary conversationalist. Despite using interpreters, Shinzo's understanding of English ensured a steady flow to our conversation. Importantly, he was able to pick up the tone and nuance of what I was saying. This helped us really understand each other. Right from the start, he chose to call me by my nickname, ScoMo, as a mark of our close relationship. This habit was picked up by Shinzo's successors. During the first in-person meeting of what is known as the Quadrilateral Security Dialogue (Quad) in the White House, which brings together the leaders of Australia, Japan, the United States, and India to address issues within the Indo-Pacific region, interpreters were baffled when Shinzo's successor, Prime Minister Suga, constantly referred to me as ScoMo in this very formal meeting. They had no idea what it meant or who it referred to.

Having established a strong foundation for our relationship at that first dinner, I often sought out Shinzo's perspective on issues. We would meet at the various international forums we were attending or catch up by phone. This continued even after he left office, including joining me for lunch in my hotel suite when I visited Japan to meet with his successor, Prime Minister Suga. After I left office,

I visited Tokyo again with Jen. Prime Minister Fumio Kishida and his wife, Yuko, kindly hosted us for breakfast at their residence. On that visit I had also been looking forward to seeing my friend Shinzo once again. But the week before we arrived, he was assassinated, and I learned that he had been speaking with his adviser only the day before he was killed to make arrangements for us to have lunch. His loss was devastating.

While leaders of nations must act in their national interest, strong personal relationships can advance shared interests where they exist. As Shinzo and I talked in 2018, there were a number of sticking points that were proving difficult to resolve. The Japanese are very polite negotiators. They don't like to say no, especially to a friend, so they tend to smile and say nothing. I asked our ambassador if a personal appeal to Shinzo would break the deadlock. He thought it might. I sat down and handwrote a personal letter to my friend, appealing to our mutual interest, the trust we had established, and the necessity of our shared future. Australia and Japan had to be closer. This was true not just to resist a more assertive China but also to better inform and balance the engagement of Western allies and partners in our region, including the United States, through initiatives like the Quad.

The agreement added another layer of depth and trust to our relationship. It would take a further two Japanese prime ministers (Suga and Kishida), a visit to Japan in the middle of COVID, and several quarantines before we finally completed the agreement. However, it would not have been possible without the initial relationship established with Shinzo and what he had taught me about patience, humility, and being steadfast to your purpose. Shinzo never made anything about himself; it was always about the partnership, the relationship, and the goal. That was his secret to getting so much done: it wasn't about him.

FOLLOW JESUS

While it is good to have heroes and mentors, we should never idolize or rely solely on them. They are not perfect. They will inevitably disappoint us if we expect too much of them. They are just human beings and are subject to the same imperfections and vulnerabilities as the rest of us.

In his first letter to the Corinthians, Paul sounded a warning about this to the local church. He was concerned about Christians getting carried away with their support for particular teachers and pastors, including himself (1 Corinthians 1:11). Celebrity pastors were a thing back then also. He said it was causing needless division in their local Christian community. Paul essentially asked, "Don't you know these guys are just human? Why are you selling yourselves so short by choosing to follow us?"

Paul said none of us are in any position to boast about anything before God. Instead, he said, "Let the one who boasts, boast in the Lord" (1 Corinthians 1:31). We can be inspired and encouraged by sound teaching, good character, and the faithful examples of people in our lives, but they are not Jesus and not who we should follow. We follow Jesus.

When I became prime minister, the media made a big deal about the fact that I was apparently Australia's first Pentecostal PM. That is not how I saw my faith nor my prime ministership. Christian denominations were created on earth, not in heaven. I follow Jesus, not any particular Christian denomination. And my faith is not my politics; it is my life. Together with my family, I have been part of a wonderful local Christian community for over fifteen years. It happens to be a mainstream evangelical Pentecostal church, but Jen and I have been part of many different Christian communities over the course of our lives. I like any church that believes the gospel, follows Jesus, loves God, loves others, is driven by faith, and wants to share the good news of the gospel. If that's your church, then we go to the same church, regardless of what it says on the front door—Orthodox, Catholic, Protestant, Reformed, evangelical, whatever.

The amazing difference between Jesus and any mortal person you may choose to follow is that if you choose to follow Jesus, His Holy Spirit actually lives within you (2 Corinthians 13:5; Ephesians 3:17–19; 1 John 4:13). No mortal hero can do this. No one can. This is what makes Christianity so different. It has the radical truth of God living within us, made possible by the sacrifice of Jesus Christ and the indwelling of the Holy Spirit. This is really out there and has no equivalence with any other religious faith or teaching.

The Bible teaches us that this can be accessed only through the action of our faith, and not just any faith but a faith in the gospel of Jesus Christ and nothing less. As Christians, we don't just try to follow Jesus' teachings, such as loving our neighbor as ourselves (Matthew 22:39; Mark 12:31; Luke 10:27). Jesus was not just a rabbi who went about with handy hints for good living. If that sums up your relationship with Jesus, you don't get it. Thinking that we can be made right with God by living a good life and even going to church denies the very heart of what the gospel message of Jesus Christ is all about. This attitude arrogantly says, "I can get there on my own, thanks. I don't really need God."

Christianity has nothing to do with how good we are or what we try to do to set things right between us and God. It is about how God took the initiative to bridge that gap between us, not the other way around. It is about recognizing where we stand with God and the sinful condition we all share, no matter who we are. We might think we're good people, we're doing our best, and we're committed to good causes. We may be happy to accept Jesus as a teacher, but what about as Savior? That might be religion, but it's not Christianity. Nicodemus had this problem.

Nicodemus was a respected and senior rabbi and priest during Jesus' time. He was known to be a good, wise, and knowledgeable man who was discerning and sensitive to the things of God. For this reason he wanted to meet Jesus. He discerned there was something different and special about Him. When Nicodemus met Jesus one night he said to Him, "We know that You have come from God as a teacher" (John 3:2). That was a nice and respectful thing to say, but Jesus cut him short and went to the heart of what He knew Nicodemus needed to understand. Jesus replied, "Unless someone is born again he cannot see the kingdom of God" (John 3:3). In an instant Jesus flipped everything Nicodemus had known about religion on its head. You can't be reconciled to God through your own natural efforts. No one can. You can do this only by becoming a new creation, being born again, through the Spirit of God, made possible by what God is doing right now through Jesus.

In the Bible's most famous verse, Jesus went on to tell Nicodemus exactly what it was that God was doing, explaining, "For God so loved the world, that He gave His only Son, so that everyone who believes in Him will not perish, but have eternal life" (John 3:16). And He did not stop there. He said, "For God did not send the Son into the world to judge the world, but so that the world might be saved through Him" (v. 17). The Jews believed that when the Messiah came He would judge the world, redeem the Jews for their faithfulness in obeying God's law, and end their oppression at that time under the Romans. Jesus said, "The one who believes in Him is not judged" (v. 18), not the one who had tried to follow all God's laws and the teachings of the prophets. Worse still, for all those who thought following the teachings was enough, "the one who does not believe has been judged already,

165

because he has not believed in the name of the only Son of God" (v. 18). Jesus said that Christianity was about the gospel—His death and resurrection for our salvation.

The Holy Spirit's indwelling within us requires a special faith in God's gospel, and in that gospel alone. It requires a faith like that of Abraham, who believed God was who He said He was and that God could do what He said He could do (Romans 4:21). Specifically, it means believing what Jesus said about Himself when He stated, "I am the way, and the truth, and the life; no one comes to the Father except through Me" (John 14:6).

In Christianity, God is the initiator through Jesus. He comes to us and says, "No more trying to fix things yourself. You can't. No more religious sacrifices that pretend to wash away your sin—they can't. No more priests who think they have to intercede between you and Me. You don't need that anymore. It's just you and Me now. What's more, I now want to move into your life and indwell you, if you'll have Me." That way, Jesus says, He can be with you every second of your life to enable you to worship, trust, talk, learn from, and have a relationship with God.

WALK HUMBLY IN LOVE

If we accept the gospel and follow Jesus, the evidence should be found in how we love others (1 John 4:20). Paul said that Jesus' dwelling within them would be built on the foundation of God's love. Paul explained that God wants Jesus to live within us through His Spirit so we can understand His love completely. Paul said, "So that Christ may dwell in your hearts through faith; and that you may be able to comprehend with all the saints [Christians] what is the width and length and height and depth, and to know the love of

Christ which surpasses knowledge, that you may be filled to all the fullness of God" (Ephesians 3:17–19).

We can expect to understand God's love only by following Jesus. To follow Jesus we must seek to be like Him. As Paul told the Philippians, we must have the same attitude as Jesus (2:5–8).

The world I served in as a politician thought only about power—how to acquire it, how to express it, how to use it (often against others), and how to hold on to it. It was not an easy place to have the same attitude as Jesus, and, I admit, at times I came up short. Paul told the Philippians that Jesus didn't think like this. He said even though Jesus knew He was God and was more powerful than everything that existed, Jesus knew that power was not the point. Jesus "did not consider equality with God something to be grasped" (Philippians 2:6). Jesus knew He didn't have anything to prove. Jesus knew He had a job to do, which was to put His own power aside to accomplish the purpose of God's love—namely, to restore our relationship with Him. Because of God's great love for us, He had chosen to fix it, not us. Jesus' purpose was love, not power. That is the example of Jesus to follow. Paul said Jesus "emptied Himself" and chose to become one of us. He "humbled Himself" and submitted Himself to death on a cross, the most shameful death imaginable. Through this extraordinary act of humility rather than power, Jesus accomplished His purpose.

Professional politics could not be further from this posture. In politics, the environment you work in is driven by competition

Jesus' purpose was love, not power.

and ambition. Our political system can also be very brutal; it's adversarial by design. Those who think things will just come to them never really make it. Doing well also makes you a target. The cut and thrust of politics can also be intoxicating. For some it can become addictive. The playing out of tactics and strategy can really test your wits and judgment. It certainly gets the adrenaline going. The danger of working in this environment is that power and the machinations of power can sometimes become more important than why you actually went into politics in the first place, and it can cloud your judgment.

This is why Jesus' example of humility was so important to me, even if I didn't always imitate it. Holding high office is not the real purpose of politics. That is the goal of selfish ambition. Getting the job of prime minister is not the achievement, nor is being popular—that comes and goes in politics. At one stage during my prime ministership, I had one of the highest domestic approval ratings of any national leader in the democratic world. On other occasions my popularity waned terribly. That's politics. It is the service that matters. Most days in the job you are a political punching bag. It goes with the territory. But you also learn to accept this as you appreciate that the job is not about you. In a representative democracy it is about those who gave you the job.

BE HOLY AS HE IS HOLY

If we say we want to follow Jesus, it must also impact how we try to live. I'm talking about our moral behavior. Being saved by grace is not a license to do whatever we want as Christians. If so, how are we any different from those who make up their own rules and try to live without God? This is an uncomfortable topic that even the church doesn't like to talk about anymore for fear of offending the prevailing "morality" of our current secular age. We're talking about sin, our language, lying, treatment of others, pride, selfishness, greed, gossip, hate, our sex lives, and the list goes on and on.

I'm not bringing this up to be self-righteous, pious, or judgmental.

Nor am I suggesting that Christians have any greater moral capacity than anyone else. Quite the opposite. Our faith should instruct us to be the most aware of our weakness in this area. I have enough sin in my own life to deal with to stay clear of judging anyone else's. It's not my business how you live your life, but it *is* God's. Holiness is not optional in following Jesus, because how you live your life affects the intimacy of your relationship with God. It affects your worship, prayer life, witness, fellowship with other Christians, and meditation on God's Word. It affects your connection with God and how you follow Him. Psalm 66:18 says, "If I regard wickedness in my heart, the Lord will not hear." I'm only raising this issue because God did. As Christians we can't kid ourselves that God doesn't care about this stuff. He does because, above all, God is holy.

God told Moses, "Be holy, because I am holy" (Leviticus 11:45). Peter quoted this same verse when he wrote to the churches in Asia (1 Peter 1:14–16). The apostle John implored Christians to purify themselves, just as Jesus was pure (1 John 3:3). Paul was explicit, instructing the Christians in Rome to present their bodies as a living and holy sacrifice, acceptable to God (Romans 12:1). He said the way we live is an act of worship to God, and he pleaded with Roman believers not to get drawn into the thinking and behavior of the secular world around them. He told them not to conform themselves to the world's thinking about what is right and wrong but instead to be transformed by the renewing of their minds (12:2). There is so much pressure on Christians today to just adopt the secular "morality" of our current age. We must resist. As Paul said to the Philippians, let your mind be the same as Jesus' (Philippians 2:5).

Peter said we used to live any which way we liked, just like the rest of the world, but now we have a reason not to (1 Peter 1:15). That reason is your relationship with God. This has nothing to do with our salvation, forgiveness, eternity, or judgment. All of that has been settled, once and for all, on the cross (Romans 6:10). Seeking to live in a way that is holy is not about achieving salvation; it's about living salvation. We do it because we value our relationship with God and we want to honor Him, worship Him, and communicate with Him. That is our purpose. We can't pretend to be in a relationship with someone we are not faithful to. Even the world knows that. Why would God expect anything different from us in our relationship with Him?

The good news is that, once again, God didn't leave us to try to achieve this on our own. He gave us the Holy Spirit to empower and enable us to be holy. This should remind us that what we do in our bodies as people who follow Jesus is no longer just about us. In the Holy Spirit we have a housemate who indwells us. God has paid the mortgage and moved in (1 Corinthians 6:19–20). Our body is now a temple of the Holy Spirit (1 Corinthians 3:16).

What you allow into your life is your business. But if we are truly sensitive to His Spirit, God will let us know when something shouldn't be there. We also don't get to change the rules about what is and isn't holy to suit ourselves or our times. We don't get to negotiate about holiness with God or put it to a vote. God is the authority on holiness. So if we truly love God and are genuine about following Jesus, we will listen to God and act on what should and shouldn't be in our lives and our behavior. It's called the conviction of the Holy Spirit.

It is also good news that if we come to God and confess our sins, we know He is faithful, and they are forgiven (1 John 1:9). We can take this to the eternity bank. This is important because we can get so disappointed with ourselves when we inevitably fail to live up to how we know God would have us to live. Sinfulness can drag us down and make us think we're no longer worthy to serve Him. This is rubbish. It doesn't change anything when it comes to where we stand with God. We must be on guard against this thinking because Satan will use it to impede our service to God.

God knows we are going to fail, but He doesn't want us to live in that failure. It's not good for us. It's not good for our relationship with Him. He also doesn't want us to live in shame or judgment. God calls Satan the accuser of God's children (Revelation 12:10). Satan will throw your sins back in your face every opportunity he can because he knows it pulls you back from your relationship with God. In stressful times Satan would often accuse me of my many sins, failings, and vanities. These transgressions were real, but God's power and forgiveness were greater. This enabled me to go forward in God's strength, not mine.

How many times have you thought that things have not turned out the way you hoped for because of sin in your life? I know I have. How could God possibly want to bless me after what I have said or how I have behaved? News flash: this is always true. God *never* wants to bless me because of what I have done for Him. Did I honestly think if I just lived better, God would reward me with special holiness points, entitling me to extra blessing? How vain is that line of thinking? That's not how God's blessing works. His blessing is an act of divine grace; it is unmerited. If I am trying to be holy just to access His blessing, then I have totally missed the point of what God is saying. We are to be holy because He is holy, not because that's how we can obtain more stuff.

God paid the price for you to leave your sin behind and not carry it forward with you.

God paid the price for you to leave your sin behind and not carry it forward with you. You can claim that promise and believe it. Don't let Satan load you up again. Thankfully the Holy Spirit that lives within us as Christians is here to help us with that. While we are often tempted, God always provides a way through (1 Corinthians

10:13) if we put on the armor of God that Paul wrote about to the Ephesians (6:10–17). That's how we follow Jesus.

REMEMBER WHO YOU ARE WITH

I love the story about the disciples in Mark 4:36–40 when Jesus calms the storm. Jesus had spent the day teaching the disciples and those gathered around Him about the kingdom of God. The disciples had just seen Jesus perform incredible miracles, raising people from the dead and healing the lame and the sick, including Peter's mother-in-law. Leaving the crowd, Jesus and His disciples went to sea. A fierce gale of wind blew up, and the waves were breaking over their boat and filling it with water. In the middle of this violent storm, Jesus was in the back of the ship, asleep on a cushion. This was an open boat being tossed about and swamped by the waves, and Jesus was fast asleep in the midst of all of it. Talk about being calm in a storm. I want to be with that guy.

In their panic the disciples woke Jesus and started accusing Him, saying, "Teacher, do You not care that we are perishing?" Notice they didn't ask for Him to save them. The disciples seemed to think this situation was beyond Jesus' control. They were amazed by Jesus' words, His teaching, and the miracles He had performed so far, but they still had no conception of who this guy really was. To be fair, the disciples were not catastrophizing. The storm was real. Waves were swamping the boat. They were genuinely terrified of losing their lives. How many times have you found yourself in that situation, swamped by the events around you, feeling there is no escape, and you think God doesn't care because all you can see is God being calm in the middle of your storm? You have listened to His teaching your entire life, but when the storm hits, you find yourself shouting at God, "Why don't You care?"

So Jesus got up, rebuked the wind, and said to the sea, "Hush, be still." When the wind died down and it all became perfectly calm, Jesus said to His disciples, "How come you guys still just don't get it?" They were amazed and said to one another, "Who is this guy?" It blew their minds. It will blow ours also when we truly understand just Who it is we have chosen to follow.

We live our lives with others. One of God's richest blessings is the people He puts in our lives. Making good choices about who we spend our lives with and follow is vital to the joy we can know in life. However, the most admirable friends, heroes, and mentors are still only human. Jesus is the only one who can provide us with ultimate assurance and security.

> *Jesus is the only one who can provide us with ultimate assurance and security.*

Throughout my life, and conscious of my human vanity, God has ensured that I have never been in any doubt that He has been the active agent in every good plan He has purposed through me. My job has been to trust and obey, regardless of the circumstances or outcome, knowing He is with me.

Part Three

WHAT SHOULD
I HOPE FOR?

Embracing Your Future

> With God, the best is always yet to come. To walk
> into the joy that God has laid up for us, we must
> learn to see the future from God's eternal perspective,
> become patient for His timing, always remember His
> past blessings, and shake off what holds us back.

Chapter Nine

WHY ARE YOU WAITING?

Wait for the LORD; be strong and let your heart
take courage; yes, wait for the LORD.

PSALM 27:14

It had not been a good few months for General George Washington. His defeat at the Battle of Brandywine, the fall of Philadelphia to the British, and a further defeat at Germantown when he sought to retake the capital had left him vulnerable. Farther north, General Horatio Gates had achieved a great victory against the British at Saratoga. Washington's detractors used Gates's success to try to have Washington removed as commander in chief.[1] Against this background, General Washington led his twelve thousand troops into Valley Forge on December 19, 1777.[2] An additional two thousand were sent to Wilmington in Delaware, while the cavalry was ordered to Trenton.[3] While the British would spend the winter months in the comforts of Philadelphia, the Continental Army would once again wait it out in the snow. During the next six months the future of Washington, the Revolution, and America would hang in the balance.

Valley Forge may not have been a battleground, but neither was it an idle place of waiting for Washington. Historian Ricardo Herrera describes Valley Forge as more like a forward operating base.[4] The ground at Valley Forge was carefully selected by Washington and his generals as the least worst option.[5] Valley Forge was set on elevated ground, aiding its defense, with the surrounding forest providing the timber to build their more permanent shelters and the firewood for their cooking and heating.[6] Valley Forge was far enough away from Philadelphia (about a day's march) to be alerted to any advance from the British but close enough not to abandon the immediate territory around the capital.[7] From here Washington could frustrate supply lines to the British, gather intelligence, and harass their outlying positions through regular patrols, where skirmishes took place. Washington sent General Nathanael Greene and up to fifteen hundred troops on an extensive foraging mission to secure supplies.[8] In February, Baron von Steuben, a Prussian military veteran of the Seven Years' War, turned up with his Russian wolfhound and turned Washington's army into a far more effective and disciplined fighting force, instituting new drills, organization, and training for the troops.[9] Valley Forge is also where Washington bonded with the Marquis de Lafayette, who had joined the Continental cause a few months before and had endured the defeats at Brandywine and Germantown, where he was wounded.[10] Lafayette would become one of Washington's most trusted generals and confidants in the years ahead.

All of this went on amid terrible deprivation. Washington lost two thousand soldiers at Valley Forge, predominantly due to starvation, disease, and exposure to the elements.[11] There were few if any blankets, and many were barefoot and without even the most basic clothing, let alone what was needed to survive a winter. During this time, Washington stayed with his army and built a strong bond with his troops, demonstrating his character and loyalty.[12] He also bonded with his officers. This would prove vital in the years that followed as he took them to ultimate victory at Yorktown. This was all done under extraordinary pressure. At the same time, Washington had to pursue the politics of war from the cramped quarters of the stone cottage he shared with his senior officers, who were also very young, including a twenty-two-year-old Alexander Hamilton.[13]

War is not just in the fighting. Dealing with politics sadly plays an enormous role in whether victory is won or lost. For Washington, this involved securing the support of a fickle Congress for his army and dealing with those who sought to undermine him and have him removed.[14] All of this he pursued through feverish correspondence throughout the winter months. At the same time, over in France, Benjamin Franklin was making progress on a treaty that would decisively change the course of the war.

In February 1778, the French entered the war, turning it into a global conflict and draining the British effort in America. Fearing a French naval blockade of Philadelphia, the British left the capital, and Washington led his army out of Valley Forge. Their waiting was over. They were now a stronger and more resilient force to be reckoned with. Washington's wait had not been in vain.

This is often the case when we are beset by challenges and it seems that all is working against us. You've lost a job; you think you'll never finish your studies; you're recovering from an illness; you're getting yourself out of debt; you can't get your business off the ground; you would love to be in a relationship but are still on your own; or your kids are constantly struggling, and you're struggling with them. Things just don't seem to be turning out the way you prayed they would.

There comes a time when, like Washington, we are forced to repair, regroup, and rebuild. We must choose our ground carefully, endure the deprivations, and remain active in the work of our survival and restoration. We build our huts, we do our drills, we scout our perimeter, we forage for supplies, and we build the bonds that will sustain us beyond our waiting. New people will come into our lives while others will depart. There will certainly be losses and further setbacks while we wait. Our response is not to lose heart and despair idly but rather to ready ourselves for the time when we know we will reemerge. Winning is often first won in the waiting.

IN THE WAITING ROOM

I am a restless soul. I like to do things. I like to be active and to constantly be on the move. If I get knocked down, I want to get straight back up again and keep moving. When I achieve something, I am the same: *What's next?* When the next thing doesn't come along on my timetable, I get frustrated.

God sees things very differently than I do. Time is not an issue for God. He has a completely different vantage point. God is eternal. He can always afford to wait. God knows the value that time adds. While I usually hate it, God often has the greatest impact on my life when He puts me in the waiting room. While it is often miserable, especially for those who have to live with me during these times, afterward, I am very thankful.

It blows my mind that God exists outside of time. He is not linear. He is the beginning, the end, and the present all at the same time. God sees the future as if it has already happened because, for God, it has. Just reflect on this for a moment and consider what this means in a practical sense. God sees our present circumstances from a future He has already secured, while at the same time building our resilience in our past so we can deal with our present. Wow. The Marvel multiverse has nothing on that.

By contrast, we can only ever see a slice of time at any one moment, and even then, not all at once. How then could we possibly comprehend eternity and the purposes of God? Good point; we can't. Given the difference between how we and God comprehend time, let alone eternity, it's probably a good idea to start trusting God more on the timing of things in our lives. In this context, what God told us about His plans for us in Jeremiah 29:11 makes even greater sense. God said His plans for us are for our prosperity and not for our disaster, to give us a future and a hope. He should know; He was in our future when He said this.

Politics could not be more foreign to this way of thinking. In politics, time is a perishable commodity. It is always in short supply. You are expected to govern with a view to the nation's best interests fifty years from now but achieve those results in just the next three. Political events are difficult to anticipate beyond a week, let alone eternity. Former British prime minister Harold Wilson is generally credited with the saying, "A week is a long time in politics."[15] He was right. A lot can change quickly in politics (and it does), so don't get too comfortable. Time will always beat you.

Being a Christian always helped me deal with the randomness and uncertainty of political life. As a follower of Jesus, I saw my eternity in God's hands, not mine, and certainly not in the hands of my political opponents, the media, or even the writers of history. The purpose of my service was to glorify God, not myself. God would be writing the only account that mattered for eternity. I understood I would serve for a season and make the best contribution I could during that time, like founding AUKUS or getting Australia through the pandemic. I would then let go and move on.

That is what stewardship is about—placing and connecting your contribution with something that endures. This requires humility. The same is true in Christian ministry. Paul explained this to the Corinthians when he wrote, "I planted, Apollos watered, but God was causing the growth" (1 Corinthians 3:6). God is the constant, not us. As a Christian in politics, I saw my role as contributing to a much bigger and longer story and trusted that God would provide the increase to my efforts. I also took encouragement from what Paul had to say about those who plant and those who water. He said each receives their own reward for the work they put in, but in doing this work they are one (3:8). Paul said we are all God's fellow workers, God's field, and God's building (3:9). I just have to do my part. I am part of what God is building, not the other way around.

I have always been bewildered by how those who do not know Jesus cope with the randomness of political life. It is true that many vainly think they can shape and control events in their favor, but they ultimately learn they are kidding themselves. Politics is like surfing—you should not confuse yourself with the wave. You didn't create the wave, nor do you control it, but you do need to learn how to catch it and ride it. There are few happy endings in politics. Most politicians are thankful to just have a happy beginning and endure the rest. So you can choose to be humble in the face of time, understanding that some sow and others reap, or you can let time humble you by thinking everything begins and ends with you. The latter approach always ends in disappointment and bitterness. I've seen this time and again.

As a follower of Jesus, you celebrate the fact that God has all the time in the world to bring about His plans and purposes through you and for you, from beginning to end, including right now. You are part of a much bigger plan. I have learned, often the hard way, that being put in the waiting room is a big part of how God achieves His purpose.

The Hebrew word that translates to our English phrase "wait for God" in Psalm 27:14 is *qavah* (pronounced kaw-vaw). It means "to wait with hope." We wait with the expectation that God will move as we spend our time actively preparing for when He does. When *qavah* is used in the Bible, God is telling us that He never asks you to wait without hope. This is big. The worst part about waiting is the feeling of hopelessness that often accompanies it. You wonder, as you feel your hopes and dreams are slipping away before you, *What is to become of us? What's going to happen? How are we going to move forward from here?* What happens if I lose? Regardless of what I think my hopes and dreams are, what I have learned is that the hopes and dreams God has for me—those plans God has for my good and not my harm that I read about in Jeremiah 29:11—never slip away. That is our hope.

The word *qavah* also implies tension—the type that causes things to strengthen, like when you are strengthening a muscle. That is why *qavah* is the word used in Isaiah 40:31 when God says, "Those who *qavah* [or wait] for the LORD will gain new strength." Our waiting extends us in our faith, producing endurance and strength that enable us to rise at the right time. This tension is the product of us wrestling with our faith. Do we really hope? Do we really trust? Can we find peace and rest in the radical idea that there is joy in suffering and waiting?

Jeremiah told us that God is good to those who put their hope in Him and that it is good to wait quietly for God (Lamentations 3:26). In my experience, Jeremiah was right, but it is harder to live than say. One of the greatest challenges for followers of Jesus is to wait in hope.

SCOMO'S FAMILY MIRACLE

Jen's dream in life was **always** to be a mum. Jen and I got married when I was just twenty-one. We were very young. There seemed to be plenty of time to have kids. After Jen had gone to college and completed her nursing degree, she went to work as a nurse at a childcare center. I was working in the private sector as a research economist.

Children love Jen. She lights up around them, and they light up around her. I would watch Jen working with kids or just being around kids with family and friends and would get so excited thinking about what an amazing mum she would be for our children one day. This was Jen's heart's desire.

In the first few years of marriage, we did what many couples do. We worked hard to get established and be in a position to buy a home, took a trip overseas, and spent time with our family and friends. We didn't immediately rush into trying to have kids, but after about four years we began trying. A couple of years went by and nothing happened. We had a problem. This was the start of an extremely difficult and often heartbreaking fourteen-year journey for us both, but particularly for Jen.

We saw everyone—fertility specialists, Chinese herbalists, naturopaths, acupuncturists, and even a fertility nun who we heard was getting good results. We were prepared to try anything and everything. We really wanted to have a family. I made some lifestyle changes, but the road for Jen was so much harder.

During my time as prime minister, Jen did some very brave things, but her bravest was to share her story about our infertility journey. For Jen it began when she was in her second year of high school. As a young girl, she experienced terrible menstrual pain. This went on for many years. In her junior year of high school, she went to see her doctor, who said it was just very strong period pains. It wasn't until she was twenty-six, following a laparoscopy, that Jen learned she suffered from stage 4 endometriosis (the worst kind).

Endometriosis is an extremely debilitating and painful condition. Up to one in ten women worldwide between the ages of fifteen and forty-four suffer from this awful condition.[16] When I saw the images of Jen's insides from the specialist, it looked like she had somehow ingested a whole tube of superglue into her reproductive system. It was a mess. Abnormal tissue builds up, causing adhesions, scarring, and cysts around the reproductive organs in the pelvis or abdomen, including the fallopian tubes, the ligaments around the uterus, the lining of the pelvic cavity, the ovaries, the outside surface of the uterus, and the space between the uterus and the rectum or bladder.[17] In one interview Jen shared what it was like, saying, "I would get so sick . . . vomiting, diarrhea, terrible backache, really extreme cramps . . . you can get pain down your legs, and everything."[18] I would watch Jen go through this every month. We started dating when Jen was seventeen. Each month, I would see Jen almost shut down. As always, she would put on a brave face and push through the pain to do whatever she needed to do at the time. Jen doesn't complain. She deals with what comes her way and gets on with it. She's one of the toughest people I know.

As if the physical pain and debilitation were not enough, studies show that 24 to 50 percent of women with infertility have endometriosis.[19] It is the most common link to female infertility. Now, this doesn't mean you can't have children, but depending on how bad the condition is, the pathway to having children gets a whole lot narrower. Mild cases may cause temporary infertility and can be overcome by surgery. More extreme cases, like Jen's, mean going down the in vitro fertilization (IVF) path. So that is what we did.

Fertility treatments have come a long way since we began our first cycle thirty years ago, back in the early nineties. When we were going through them, they were more likely to fail than succeed, and they were expensive then too. While the opportunity to have access to such treatment is an extraordinary blessing, especially in Australia, where it is partially supported financially by our health system, IVF can still feel like a very dehumanizing process. As a Christian—believing that a child should be the result of the natural expression of love between a man and woman in a lifelong partnership of marriage—IVF can make you feel like you've been reduced to a biology project. Jen became a pincushion. Her stomach looked like she'd just played a game of rugby and been kicked repeatedly in the stomach. The drugs took her on an emotional roller-coaster ride. The male contribution to the IVF process was also a bit awkward.

Now, don't get me wrong, I am amazed at the science that makes this possible and am thankful for it and for the financial support fertility treatments receive in Australia. I never had any ethical, moral, or religious concerns over our IVF treatments. God gave us creativity and intellectual capacity for a reason. Science is the product of that gift, not its opponent. I have always found in science reasons to praise God, not doubt God.

During the next fourteen years, we underwent ten cycles of IVF. Every one of them failed. It is hard to describe the mental torture of waiting to hear the results of each progressive stage of the process. First we had to "harvest" the eggs and the sperm. They were then fertilized together in a lab. We then waited anxiously to see if they "took." Sometimes this process would fail, yielding nothing. This was before the internet and text messaging, so we would wait for a call from the clinic. I really felt for the nurses (who were amazing) at these clinics who had to make these calls. When the news was negative, our hearts sank. We felt numb.

For me, my own disappointment was nothing compared to seeing Jen's heartbreak. The disappearance of hope is a soul-destroying thing to watch, particularly in the person you love more than any other in the world. There is nothing you can do to take away the pain or despair. We would just hold each other if we were together when the news came through. We would cry and grieve.

Throughout this time, we had wonderful and supportive family and friends. Jen especially had her close girlfriends. We couldn't have made it through without them, but we also used to dread having to tell them about the results. They didn't want to hear bad news, and we didn't want to tell them. This is often why you don't want to tell people you are doing IVF. It wasn't just because it was a private matter; you just didn't want to risk having to share the news with anyone if it failed. It was like reliving the moment again. If we got a positive report and the egg or eggs fertilized, then we went on to the next stage. The success rate after eggs being implanted was about one in three back then, so we tended to double down and implant multiple embryos and play the percentages. It is terrible to talk about these things in this way, but that is just one of the many dehumanizing elements of going through IVF.

That next wait was even more excruciating. We often didn't tell friends and family if we had gotten to the next stage, as it added unnecessary pressure. At this point we would just wait to see if Jen had her next period and pray.

Jen prayed for a child the way Hannah prayed for Samuel: in despair and in tears. Hannah pleaded that God would look on her affliction and remember her (1 Samuel 1:10–11). One day God's priest, Eli, saw Hannah praying, and he was watching her mouth. The Bible says Hannah was speaking in her heart with only her lips quivering. Eli thought she was drunk, but Hannah said, "No, . . . I am a woman despairing in spirit; I have . . . poured out my soul before the LORD" (1 Samuel 1:13). I could not describe Jen's heart during these times any better than that.

I remember one particular cycle when we had two embryos implanted and we allowed ourselves to hope. We named them and waited expectantly for their arrival. They didn't make it. We were crushed. We felt forgotten by God. We cried again until we ran out of tears. It says in Psalm 126:5 that those who sow in tears shall harvest with joyful shouting. At this point, all we knew were the tears. We learned of the failure of this cycle while we were away together in the Blue Mountains west of Sydney, while staying at my parents' holiday house in Blackheath for the weekend. We went out to the local plant nursery and bought two small camellia shrubs and planted them in the garden in memory of the children we never got to meet. Throughout the process, one thing we were convinced of was that every embryo that failed was one of our children and that one day in heaven we would meet them all for the first time. We are both looking forward to that day when they will greet us.

This went on time and again. We prayed with elders. We were anointed with oil. We cried out to God to remember us.

I remember vividly one day when we were living in Wellington, New Zealand, and I was walking through the greenbelt that surrounds the city. I was furious with God, but not just on my account. I was furious with Him for what Jen was going through. I knew only too well my failings of faith, but how could He allow Jen to suffer like this? Having children was the great desire of Jen's heart. It was the most selfless desire you could imagine. This was not selfish ambition; this was the selfless desire of love. Only God could have put such a pure desire in her heart. I screamed Psalm 37:4 in Jen's defense: "You say 'Trust in the LORD and do good. . . . Delight yourself in the LORD; and He will give you the desires of your heart.' Here she is, here am I, God, pleading the earnest desire of our hearts, and yet You do not remember us!" If anyone was in earshot, they must have thought I was a madman. My heart was broken, and my spirit was crushed.

That was 1999. Our journey was not even half over.

Two miracle daughters later, when I think back to that day, I am struck by how this must have been heartbreaking for God also. See, when we are in the waiting room, we think it is only us there feeling the pain, frustration, and sorrow. But God knows and feels that pain with us. God was there walking with me in that forest, seeing my pain and anguish, yet at the same time was looking from our future at the hope He had already laid up for us. I can now hear Him saying, *Scott, if you only knew what is ahead. I'm here now. I can see it. You should see your faces and those of your children. Please know I would never forget or forsake you. I need you to know that, especially at times like this when you're hurting. I know this is stretching you. I know it's hard, but please push through in faith. Now is not yet time for Abbey and Lily to come into your lives, but that time is coming, and you will rejoice, and we will laugh and cry together in great joy, just as I did with Abraham and Sarah. They also had to wait. Believe Me, My plans are for your good, not your harm. I love you.*

I would learn the truth of Psalm 22 where, although starting with "God, my God! Why have you forsaken me?" the psalmist ends with "He has never let you down, never looked the other way when you were being kicked around. He has never wandered off to do his own thing; he has been right there, listening" (vv. 1, 23–24 MSG).

Over the next few years, we would try again and again without success. One day our fertility specialist told us he no longer thought it was going to happen for us. There was nothing further he could do. This broke Jen. Living with infertility can be a marriage breaker. It puts so much emotional and financial stress on a relationship. It sucks up every bit of oxygen. It is the background to every conversation and qualification on every plan. It is like an oppressive but unseen mist. Of course I still wanted children, but I didn't want this to rob us of our life together. I tried to reassure Jen that our life would be no less full if our dream wasn't able to be realized. Together, our cup would always be full.

We tried to move on, but Jen never gave up. It was impossible for her. A few years later, in 2004, a friend suggested we see another doctor who believed we still had a chance. This led to Jen undergoing extensive surgery to clear her endometriosis, which included resecting part of her bowel. The endometriosis had also spread to Jen's liver. Surgery to remove the adhesions on such sensitive organs could cause serious long-term damage. The surgery took five hours.

The following day Jen started to hemorrhage and was losing a lot of blood. A pastor from the church we were attending at the time came to the hospital and prayed for Jen. She went back into surgery that night. I have never seen her look more fragile in my entire life. I was so worried that our quest to have children may now cost us everything. I sat in her room at the hospital. She did not receive many visitors, as she needed to rest and recover. We waited; she slept and I prayed. Thankfully, Jen made a full recovery.

Over the next few years, we tried IVF a few more times at a new clinic but were sadly unsuccessful. In mid-2006, I lost my job at Tourism Australia, and we moved to the Shire to wait for an opportunity to run for Parliament. God had put me back in the waiting room. I no longer had the stress of a demanding job and was living a much healthier lifestyle. I took up kayaking and got fit. Jen and I were spending a lot more time together. Within just a few months, our miracle happened. Three years after Jen's surgery— after fourteen years of trying, ten failed IVFs, and one successful microsurgery—she fell pregnant naturally. We could not contain our joy. We waited three months before deciding to share the news with our close family and friends.

It was almost Christmas, and all our family had come over for lunch. At our Christmas gatherings we like to have bonbons. We call them Christmas Crackers. Two people each hold a separate end and pull the paper fuse, which creates a loud bang. You then open them to find a small child's toy and a bit of paper with the worst possible collection of dad jokes printed on them to share with the table. Jen and I had snuck copies of the ultrasound image into the crackers instead. We'd photoshopped a little red Santa hat onto the baby's head. It looked very cute.

When everyone sat down, we were very keen for them to do their Christmas Crackers. For such a routine tradition, no one could quite understand our urgency. They finally got around to it. We waited and watched them open up their crackers and unfold the paper with the ultrasound image. There were shrieks of joy and disbelief as everyone seemed to get what was going on, except for my dad, who was completely clueless. Mum and my brother, Alan, explained it to him, and he broke down in tears. My dad had been a policeman for his entire working life. He was always the one who held it together, no matter what happened. But he could not hold back his joy. As I remember these scenes now, I think again of how this is what God would have been seeing seven years before as I was unloading my heart on Him as I walked through the forest in Wellington. But it would get even better.

One Friday morning in July, Jen and I woke up and her water broke. We contacted the hospital, and they made plans for us to come into the birthing suite later that day. There was no mad dash; there was plenty of time. We arrived in the early afternoon and got settled. Things were proceeding slowly. Around 8:00 p.m., after the epidural, Jen was having a rest. A few hours later, things started to get busy. As midnight approached, Jen was in full labor. There were signs the baby was in distress. Suddenly there were many people in the room, and the obstetrician and midwives worked urgently to get Abbey out safely. And then, the miracle. Abbey was born on the seventh day of the week (Saturday), on the seventh day of the month, in the seventh month of the year, in the year 2007: 07/07/07. Seven is God's number of completeness and perfection. I just love how God pays attention to the details. There was no way we could ever doubt the source of our blessing. Abigail means "father's joy" in Hebrew, and we called her Abbey for short. She was our first miracle child.

About eighteen months later, when I was a member of Parliament, I was in our bedroom one morning when Jen walked in holding something in her hand that I couldn't make out. Just when I thought my cup could not be more full, Jen handed me a pregnancy test with two straight lines on it. I burst out laughing, not in disbelief but in pure joy. My cup now ran over. In June 2009, Lily was born. She was our second miracle girl. I have kept that pregnancy test to this day. How good is God!

Our story had a happy ending. That is not the case for all couples who struggle with infertility, but thankfully the science is a lot better than it used to be. The point of recounting this story is not to suggest that someone else's story will end the same. I don't know. I do know, though, that God traveled the entire journey with us and that whatever future we had in store, He had gone ahead to prepare it. God is always in the waiting.

In our last annual budget while I was prime minister, I was able to introduce a new funding program to support the eight hundred thousand women in Australia who suffer from endometriosis. This new program established a series of clinics around the country, provided funding for MRI scans to assist with detection and diagnosis, increased resources for research, and boosted clinical training and assistance with pain management for sufferers. I announced the funding plan at one of our larger hospitals in Sydney. In concert with the announcement, Jen had done a series of interviews talking bravely about her own experience. As we stood together making the announcement, I was so pleased that, for at least once, Jen could see how our journey together through this ordeal had resulted not just in our own blessing but in the opportunity to make life a bit easier for others. Blessed to be a blessing. These are the precious moments of political service. It was a long time in the waiting.

Almost a year after leaving office following the election loss, Jen and I were at the opening night of *Madame Butterfly*. The opera was being performed on our harbor waterfront with the Sydney Opera House and Harbour Bridge as the backdrop, in the open air on a magnificent fall evening. It is a truly stunning annual event. Afterward we attended the reception and were chatting with various people when two young women approached Jen and thanked her for her bravery for opening up about her endometriosis. They both suffered from it and were just thankful that someone in Jen's position had seen them and acknowledged what they went through and had been able to bring about some change. Jen responded humbly to them, asked about their own stories, and listened carefully. I just stood there looking at Jen, listening to her encourage these young women and being thankful for the amazing blessing she has been in my life, for her strength, faith, humility, and, above all, a love that never gives up in the waiting.

A LIFE OF PREPARATION

God will put us through many seasons of waiting in our lives, but it will never be without purpose. God never wastes a wait—just ask Joseph of Arimathea. Isaiah 53:9 says of Jesus' burial that "His grave was assigned with wicked men, yet He was with a rich man in His death, because He had done no violence, nor was there any deceit in His mouth." Joseph of Arimathea was that rich man.

The events of Jesus' crucifixion, death, burial, and resurrection are extraordinary. What if He had not suffered such a public death? Some may have said that He had been released and had fled into exile; others may have claimed His disciples helped Him escape. What if the soldier had not thrust the spear into His side? If not for this act, people might have claimed that Jesus recovered in the tomb. What if Jesus hadn't been buried in a tomb with a big stone in front of it? I recall listening to a sermon from Pastor Caleb Treat of Christian Faith Center in Seattle in which he said that Jesus didn't need the stone rolled away to get out of the tomb, as Jesus could walk through walls. The stone was rolled away for our benefit. All

God never wastes a wait.

of these events happened in such a way, and in accordance with Old Testament prophecy, for the gospel to be declared and for Jesus to have the greatest impact of any life in human history. This is incredible. Jesus' ministry lasted for just three years. He did not leave behind any writings by His own hand. At any point, Jesus' story could have been lost to history. This is particularly the case when it came to His death and resurrection, especially what they did with Jesus' body. Thankfully, God was paying attention to the details.

Crucifixion was the execution of choice for the lowest of the low. It was a shameful death and intended to be so. Crucifixion was an obscenity. At that time if you wished to abuse or offend someone, you could probably have told them to "get crucified." I'll leave it to your imagination how this would translate into today's colorful language.

Usually after a crucifixion, the body would be left to rot in place on the cross to be devoured by vultures and wild animals. The whole point of crucifixion was to serve as a warning to others. In some cases, bodies would be taken down and burned and only occasionally buried. However, even taking the time to dig a mass grave was usually considered too much effort. Those executed by crucifixion were seen as completely worthless, devoid of all human dignity. That said, it was also Roman law not to refuse families if they petitioned to be given the body.

There were good arguments for the Jewish leaders not to allow Jesus' body to be left to rot on the cross, as the Sabbath was approaching. Although they had opposed Jesus, they also knew that many had heard His teachings and saw Him as a teacher or rabbi. He had been teaching to large crowds all week in the temple during the busiest time of the year. To allow His body to be desecrated and not properly buried could blow back on them. The Romans also didn't need a scene. Better to have someone take care of the body. Enter Joseph of Arimathea.

We know from the Gospels that Joseph was a member of the Jewish Council and a secret disciple of Jesus, like Nicodemus. We also know that he was a rich man (Matthew 27:57). Joseph would have known how things worked in Jerusalem. He would have had contacts. He would have known what to do, who he needed to talk to, and how to fill out the paperwork. Furthermore, he had the means to do so. In particular, he had a burial place that he had already purchased, with a great big stone that could be rolled in front of it to seal the tomb (John 19:41). I believe none of this happened by accident.

Joseph's entire life up until this moment had prepared him for this great and courageous act of service. As Joseph grew up, he would have become familiar with the teachings of the Jewish faith.

When he came into adulthood, he would have taken on positions of service and leadership as he rose to become a member of the council. This would have taken many years of devoted service, gaining the respect, trust, and admiration of his peers. Through his exposure to the Scriptures and God's teachings, Joseph's eyes would have been progressively opened to the prophecies and teachings about the Messiah. While we do not read about the source of Joseph's wealth, we can imagine how for decades Joseph would have received God's favor. In every deal and every venture that enhanced his position, there was God. The skills he needed to build and maintain his wealth would have been the product of so many experiences where God had guided his hand, including through failings and disappointments.

As Joseph heard the accounts of Jesus and likely heard Him speak firsthand in the temple, he would have begun to realize just who Jesus was. His quiet realization would lead him to step up on the night of Jesus' crucifixion. Joseph's life of faithfulness had prepared him for this exact moment. Its significance is hard to underestimate. Without a secure tomb, there would be no credible resurrection story. Joseph's role was arguably one of the most important actions of anyone in the Gospels.

It's probably true Joseph had no idea of the significance of what he was doing at the time. He was just acting in obedience to what he thought to be the right thing to do as a follower of Jesus. While he had kept this to himself, it was now time to take a risk for his genuinely held belief.

Our time on earth, when set against eternity, is quite short. In Psalm 103:15–16 our days are compared to flowers in the field, resplendent one day and chaff the next. Only our faith and how we live for God's glory last—how we love, how we forgive, how we honor God in our lives. This is what Joseph did. After a lifetime of patient and faithful service, honoring God, being sensitive to His Word, and fulfilling his role as a faithful steward, he was ready, and he acted in faith.

When we wait with Jesus through every day and every season and every sorrow, we ensure that whatever God requires of us each day, whether humble and selfless acts of uncommon love or grand acts of state, is the result of us being ready. That readiness is the product of the seasons of life God has taken us through during the course of our lives. That is where the living happens.

Chapter Ten

WHAT'S HOLDING
YOU BACK?

*"And forgive us our debts, as we also
have forgiven our debtors."*
MATTHEW 6:12

The Tamworth Country Music Festival is Australia's equivalent
of Nashville's CMA Fest. Each year, on our national day weekend in late January—at the height of Australian summer—country
music artists, fans, and tourists gather at Tamworth in the north-
west of New South Wales to celebrate the best of Australian country
music. Back in 1991, a young Australian artist won his first Golden
Guitar award (like a Grammy or CMA Award) for recording the
song "I Never Work on a Sunday."[1] In 1992 he won two more
Golden Guitars.[2] His name is Keith Urban. You may have heard
of him. Jen and I are big fans. He comes from a long line of great
Australian country artists. These awards have also consistently

recognized the unique talent of Australia's Aboriginal country music artists. Probably the best known is Jimmy Little, who passed away in 2012. If you asked Australians who the first Aboriginal was to win a Golden Guitar, they would probably say Jimmy Little. But it's actually not true; it was a young man named Col Hardy who grew up in the small outback town of Brewarrina, which was home to just a few hundred people.[3] Col is now in his early eighties and has lived in the Shire for decades.

I first met Col when I became involved in the Clontarf Foundation. Clontarf works with Aboriginal boys in our schools to provide them with positive male mentors. These mentors help the boys stay in school, get healthy, and learn respect for themselves, each other, their community, and their culture. Clontarf uses the boys' love of sports to keep them engaged. When the program was expanded from Western Australia to my home state of New South Wales, they came to see me, and I got on board immediately. An academy program was commenced at Endeavour High School in the Shire, which was run by Col's son Jeff. Since that time, I have been pleased to help them in any way I can. This included securing significant federal budget funding when I was treasurer and prime minister. This enabled Clontarf to triple the size of its program from supporting around three thousand boys each year to more than twelve thousand.

Col left Brewarrina in his early twenties to pursue his music career in Sydney. He overcame the extraordinary adversity of growing up in an Australia that didn't recognize indigenous people as citizens or count them in our census, let alone give them a vote. But you won't find a hint of bitterness in Col. You will observe a kind and gentle spirit that tells and sings the stories of his people and our country.

On one Clontarf trip, I visited Brewarrina with Col. He took us to see the Aboriginal fish traps on the Barwon River. They are a series of ancient low stone walls constructed in the river, running around half a kilometer. Fish would be herded and trapped in the complex array of weirs and pens created by the stone walls as they migrated upriver. The permanent construction was strong enough to weather high and low river flows. No one knows how old the fish traps are, but according to Australia's National Heritage Register, they are probably at least three thousand years old and possibly even fifteen thousand years old.[4] Col used to come down to the traps when he was a boy. As I stood in the outback heat with Col that day, a gentle breeze played with the leaves of the ghost gums lining the bank. I imagined the ancient scenes of people building and maintaining the traps over centuries, their children playing on the banks and in the small pools, splashing each other as their parents gathered the fish and took them back to camp. It was hard to reconcile this image with the horrifying and violent one that occurred just on the other side of the river, in a colonial massacre, centuries later.

In my maiden speech to Parliament when I was first elected as an MP, I argued that it was important that we tell the truth about Australia's history. I said we must celebrate our incredible achievements but also acknowledge the terrible stains of our past, especially concerning the treatment of our indigenous peoples. The good does not cancel the bad, nor does the bad cancel the good. It is a complex narrative. People are complex, and so are nations. Stories of dispossession and violence against indigenous peoples are not unique to Australia, but this makes them no less inexcusable. You will find similar terrible stories in every country that emerged from colonization.

In 1928, an article appeared in a Sydney newspaper recounting a brutal massacre of Aboriginal people at Hospital Creek near Brewarrina in 1882.[5] The article provided a firsthand account of the massacre by its perpetrator, Con Bride. It included many of the hallmarks of violence carried out against indigenous peoples by colonizers across the world.

There was no justification for the massacre, even though Con tried to offer one. This atrocity, and many like it, was a terrible stain on our nation. We cannot pretend they didn't occur or seek to rationalize them, as Con attempted. We should be horrified, outraged, appalled, and ashamed. I am all of these, both as an Australian and as a Christian. This was the dark side of colonization that is regrettably part of our nation's story. As a nation founded on Judeo-Christian values, particularly the belief in the inherent dignity of every human being, our future depends on coming to terms with these stories.

PRAYER OF CONFESSION

It was one of my first weeks in Parliament. Even though my party had just lost the election and we would spend the next six years in opposition, I was still excited to finally be there. A new Labor government had been elected with Kevin Rudd as prime minister. One of his first acts was to offer a historic apology to Aboriginal and Torres Strait Islander peoples for the past practice of forcibly removing children from their parents to be raised by adoptive families or in state-sanctioned institutions. In practice, it became a national apology for all the injustice, indignity, deprivation, and violence, like the Hospital Creek Massacre, suffered by indigenous Australians for more than two centuries.

The apology was not a substitute for the hard work and difficult choices needed to reduce indigenous disadvantage. It would not materially change any of the hardships being experienced by indigenous Australians. However, to confine the apology to an exercise in symbolism misses the point. While symbols are important in informing and transforming culture, I believed there was more at work here. I felt there was spiritual significance to what was taking place. I saw the apology as a spiritual act of national repentance. I believe Kevin did also. But I can't pretend this was a universal view.

When the apology was offered, large numbers of indigenous Australians traveled to Canberra. They camped on the grounds and gathered on Parliament's lawns, looking at large screens as the apology was given. They cried, they held each other, and they rejoiced. The benefit, however, was not just for them. The need for repentance can be a great stumbling block to any personal or national journey. Our regrets and our past can hold us back. To move forward and address the practical challenges of eliminating indigenous disadvantage (or closing the gap, as it became known), we had to confront our past. Kevin was right. We had to acknowledge what had occurred. It had to be brought into the light. We had to prosecute the case and accept the verdict that these actions were wrong and had caused terrible damage to the lives of fellow Australians. We then had to take responsibility as a society and repent of these practices.

Why? What good was this? What was to be gained? My answer was the hope of our own healing and restoration. Kevin's actions put this within reach.

Some years later, when Kevin was no longer in office, he joined me and a few other colleagues at our regular Tuesday night Bible study in my office at Parliament. That night we discussed Kevin's apology, and Kevin shared with us his Christian theological framework for the speech. Kevin had crafted the apology as a national statement of spiritual repentance. It was a prayer.

Kevin and I shared a friendship with Bruce Baird, who was my predecessor in my parliamentary seat of Cook. He was a mentor for many years. I remember when Kevin won the election, Bruce said to me, "Just because you disagree with Kevin's politics, do not discount the fact that God can also work His purposes through him and his side of politics." He said this with a smile to tease me, but it was also penetrating wisdom. While there would be many times I would disagree with Kevin, and he would return the favor when I was PM, there was no doubt God used him powerfully to bring about the historic apology. This will be forever to his credit.

HOPE OF FORGIVENESS

Fourteen years later, I delivered a speech as PM in Parliament to mark the anniversary of Kevin's original apology. On that first occasion, Kevin had rightly highlighted repentance as a prerequisite for reconciliation. I reinforced this principle. I said we remained sorry as a nation for the ruthless laws that broke apart families and for brutalities masked as protection and compassion. We remained sorry for the lives damaged and destroyed. On this occasion, however, I thought it was time to revisit another Christian principle essential for reconciliation—namely, forgiveness.

While true repentance cannot expect, let alone demand, forgiveness, there is still hope for mercy. There is still the prayer that grace may abound and transcend the weighing of hurts and grievances. Forgiveness is an act of grace and courage. It is a gift that only the wounded, damaged, or destroyed can offer. Forgiveness also carries a price. When we forgive, we forgo the payment we are owed for the hurt we have suffered. We choose to bear the cost of that injury ourselves. "I'm sorry" is not the hardest thing to say; "I forgive" is.

The possibility of forgiveness opens up the opportunity for

restoration and release from the pain and suffering that no apology can achieve. I argued that forgiveness in the context of the historic injury done to indigenous peoples was not a call for a national statement of forgiveness from Australia's indigenous peoples. It is inconceivable how such a statement could even be credibly formulated. No, forgiveness would need to rest with each individual. Forgiveness must be a true statement from the individual's heart. It could not be delegated to a collective, nor could it be expected or demanded. However, without it, I believed true reconciliation would never be achieved.

> *Forgiveness is an act of grace and courage.*

The reaction to my raising the issue of forgiveness in the context of our national reconciliation debate drew a predictable and sharp rebuke from social justice advocates. It was decried as insensitive. I strongly disagreed. Forgiveness did not mean the denial of consequences. As prime minister, I completed the outstanding settlement agreement for indigenous peoples impacted by the policies of forced removal in the Australian Capital Territory. For most social justice advocates, however, forgiveness was a step too far. Yet that has not always been the case.

No one would credibly challenge the late Archbishop Desmond Tutu's social justice credentials. When seeking reconciliation in South Africa, he urged, "Let us go . . . the Christian way, the way that says, yes there is a risk in offering people forgiveness; you don't know how they are going to turn out. But that's not . . . our business, that God's business, with that particular individual. There is a need for understanding but not for vengeance, a need for reparation but not for retaliation, a need for ubuntu[6] but not for victimization."[7] Tutu's biographer explained that "the person who had ubuntu [which roughly translates as 'the belief in a universal bond of sharing that connects all humanity'[8]] was known to be compassionate and gentle, who used his strength on behalf of the weak, who did not take advantage of others—in short he cared, treating others as what they were, human beings."[9] Reverend Martin Luther King Jr. advocated the same approach.

Timothy Keller wrote in his book *Forgive* that notions of justice and forgiveness have become irreconcilable in today's secular morality.[10] Yet our God is still the God of justice and forgiveness, having reconciled both in Himself through Jesus Christ on the cross. This idea is an offense to every instinct of modern "morality" and is strongly resisted.

In rejecting forgiveness, today's justice campaigners have become the fire-and-brimstone preachers of cancellation and banishment. They argue that forgiveness only empowers the perpetrator, denies justice, and therefore puts others at risk. There is some truth to this in the way that the doctrine of forgiveness has been abused, especially by the church, to protect perpetrators of abuse. Victims were bullied into silence by the church leveraging their faith against them, protecting those who were in desperate need of repentance themselves from being exposed for their crimes. With victims silenced, perpetrators continued their abuse. This is shameful, and it cheapened the true power and purpose of forgiveness. But it is not a reason to abandon the true doctrine of forgiveness that Jesus taught.

Forgiveness is like repentance in many ways except one: forgiveness is the victim's domain, while repentance is the perpetrator's. Neither the victim nor the perpetrator can do the other's job, but they do follow similar processes. Like with repentance, in offering forgiveness, a victim must not diminish the offense and injury to themselves, at least in their own consciousness. You forgive and repent of offenses that are real, where the injury is real, and where the consequences are real. For those needing repentance, Keller reminded us you may be able to get away with your sin, but you can't get away from it.[11] This is also true for those who need to forgive. We can look away from our hurt, but we cannot get away from it. These hurts hold on to us, whether we are conscious of it or not. These hurts are also organic. Either we let them live and grow, or we kill them and they die.

It's also essential to understand the difference between forgiveness and justice. While you have the power to forgive your perpetrator, the responsibility for judgment is appropriately determined by those who have the authority to do so, be that human or divine justice. Being a victim does not give us the authority to sit in the judgment seat, whether this is God's throne or a judge's seat on the bench.

When crimes are committed and laws are broken, judgment is a matter for our human justice system. This does not negate human forgiveness. By forgiving, you release the offender from your vengeance and malice. But this does not alter whether a crime has been committed or laws have been broken. Crimes and the breaking of laws are not just offenses against the individual. They are offenses against society, for which there are consequences. That is why, in civil society, crimes should be reported and prosecuted in a justice system governed by rules of fairness and procedure, where judgment is determined dispassionately and not arbitrarily. Too often today, we see social media displace our courts as the means to dispense justice. Why bother with all the paperwork when "justice" activists and commentators have already judged their targets guilty? A conviction is easier to achieve in the media, or social media. Who needs the courts? The zeitgeist has spoken. This strikes me as just another form of tyranny.

Our courts are forums not for vengeance but for upholding our laws. Justice is not meted out by the victim or the media but by the courts in accordance with and accountable to our laws. While we can and should forgive, we can also rightly relay judgment for any offense to those given the authority to render it. When we do this, it is not from a motivation for vengeance, punishment, or likes on social media but for justice, restoration, and upholding the rule of law, essential to any functional and free society. It is the same with God's eternal judgment. As Bishop Tutu said, it's God's business, not ours. Our business is forgiveness.

Social justice advocates who protest against the virtues of forgiveness run the risk of disempowering the victims they claim to be protecting. They do this by denying them the only real power they often have. They cannot force a perpetrator to repent, and while offenses can be reported, our human systems of justice are not infallible. These things are beyond our control. Forgiveness is the only real power victims truly have that is entirely within their control.

Keller said, "The heart dresses vengeance up as if it were justice."[12] You don't have to choose between forgiveness and justice, but you do have to choose between forgiveness and vengeance. You do have to choose between forgiving your offender and hating them. You do have to choose between being set free from your grievance and letting it control you. You have to choose between being open to restoration and reconciliation rather than ghosting and canceling. You have to choose to let go of the offense, whether that is not bringing it up in your thoughts or conversation or not holding it against someone as if they are on probation. You must choose to hope and pray that things go well for the one you forgive, not fantasize about their downfall or humiliation, hoping they will suffer as they made you suffer. That is not forgiveness. Forgiveness is hard, and it costs; but in forgiving, you also find blessing and the ability to move forward with God's plans for your good. Sometimes that journey can be incomprehensible.

A SUMMER EVENING'S TRAGEDY

On Saturday, February 1, 2020, we decided to shut our international border to protect the nation against COVID-19. I spent the day in meetings with our National Security Committee, state and territory leaders, and the prime minister of New Zealand. In the following weeks, the pandemic would go from bad to worse.

That was not the only thing that happened that day. That evening, across town in the leafy Sydney suburb of Oatlands, Danny and Leila Abdallah had been enjoying a hot summer's day with their six children. After their relatives arrived, the kids asked if they could go to the shops to buy some ice cream. Their parents agreed, provided the kids all stayed together.

Soon after 7:30 p.m., the children set off. Seven in all, brothers, sisters, and cousins, aged between eight and thirteen. Nothing could be more ordinary and natural than kids making their way to the shops on a hot summer evening, one of them on his bike, the older ones keeping an eye on the younger ones, as their parents had taught them.

Earlier that day, Samuel Davidson, a twenty-nine-year-old truck driver, had been at a friend's party. He had been drinking heavily and taking drugs. Samuel left the party with a friend and got into his large four-wheel-drive vehicle. At around 7:45 p.m., they were speeding down a road not far from Danny and Leila's home. They were doing over 130 km/hr (80 mph) in a 50 km/hr (30 mph) zone.

In one terrible moment, everything changed. Samuel's vehicle mounted the curb and ran into the young children from behind as they were walking along the sidewalk. Samuel kept driving up the road before he stopped. The youngest boy's bike lay twisted on the ground along the side of the road. Ambulance officers used words like *carnage*, *horrific*, *chaos*, and *senseless* to describe the scene after they arrived. Danny raced to the scene. When he arrived, he saw his children motionless on the ground under a tree. He tried to revive his son Antony. When Leila arrived, she could see them but still did not know who had survived. Danny told Leila to go with their daughter Liana, who was injured but still alive, to the hospital. Their other two daughters, Sienna and Angelina, along with Antony, had all died at the scene, along with their cousin, Veronique.

Danny later described how he saw the police cover each of his children with a white sheet. "They were gone," he said. Danny called his cousin Bridget, who was Veronique's mother. Bridget said it was strange that Danny was calling her. She answered the phone asking, "Is everything okay, Danny?" Danny said no. He told her to come to the Oatlands Golf Club. They raced to the car, and Bridget began to pray, "Hail Mary . . . Our Father . . . Hail Mary . . . Our Father . . ." Upon Bridget's arrival, the street was blocked, and there were people everywhere. Bridget started calling out loud to the people and police, "My daughter is down there, please let me in, I am her mum." Bridget begged and begged, but the police did not let her in. She sat on the sidewalk.

The audible sobs and cries of disbelief and heartbreak of family members and friends as they arrived overwhelmed the scene, disrupted only by the flashing red and blue lights of the emergency vehicles, which testified that this was not a bad dream. In the hospital, Danny would have to tell his surviving daughter, Liana, that her older brother and two sisters had been killed. It was not until Danny arrived at the hospital with three priests that Leila also realized her other children were dead. She cried and begged for it not to be true, but it was.

Danny and Leila lost three of their six children that night. Bridget lost her daughter. Her son, Michael, lost his younger sister.

At the scene Michael asked, "What am I going to do? How am I going to live the rest of my life without her?"

At the scene after the crash it is reported that Samuel was heard saying, "What have I done? I have killed people. I am going to jail."[13] When the police gave Samuel a breath test at the scene, it registered 0.15. That is three times the legal limit. Samuel was charged with more than thirty serious offenses, including manslaughter.

This is what tragedy looks like. It is raw, senseless, punishing, unrelenting, and uncompromising. One person's failure to act responsibly becomes another family's enduring and insufferable loss. Samuel's life, and that of his family, was also destroyed. But what happened next is incredible.

I4GIVE

At the crash site the next day, Danny spoke briefly to the media, but it was still too soon to put his grief into words. When Leila arrived, she had to be supported to stand. She leaned over and held on to the railing of the fence that separated the golf course from the sidewalk, where a makeshift memorial had already been established, with flowers, photos, cards, rosaries, crosses, and children's toys being laid at the site to pay tribute to the young lives lost and to show support for their families. The Christian Maronite community in this part of Sydney is very close. I have known this community for many years and love them dearly. Leila knelt as she read the cards and was inconsolable. She would later say that her grief felt like her heart was being "pierced with a sword." Bridget said she carried what seemed like "a ton of lead" in her heart.

By the following day a vigil was occuring at the crash site. Crowds gathered to pray. Danny spoke to the media about his children.

His handsome boy Antony, who loved basketball; his little helper Angelina, who always had his back; and his little "diva," Sienna. "They've gone to a better place," he said. In a statement, Bridget and her family thanked the first responders and spoke of their vibrant eleven-year-old girl, Veronique, who was full of life and love. When Leila was asked by the media for her response, she stopped the nation. This was the most incredible witness of the love of Jesus in a person's life I have ever seen. Leila said, "I cannot hate him . . . in my heart I forgive him." She then said, "But I want the court to be fair, right."

Some months later, when Leila was explaining her instinctive decision to forgive, she said, "If Jesus can forgive, we have to forgive." She later said she prayed for the driver and the passenger and everyone in need of prayer, but at the same time she said you need justice. Leila forgave the man who had killed her children less than forty-eight hours prior, but then she resolved to leave justice in the hands of those responsible for it.

All of this occurred in the first sitting week of Parliament in the new year. I was stuck in Canberra. On Tuesday morning we had our church service to open the parliamentary year. After the service I was approached by the media. My first words were to express my thoughts and prayers for the families. At this time I did not know them, but we were to become good friends.

Jen attended the funerals on my behalf—first the funerals of Antony, Angelina, and Sienna, and then, the following day, Veronique. In her loving way Jen made a real connection with Leila and Bridget and remained in contact with them following the funerals. We would later invite them to our residence at Kirribilli, where I met them for the first time. Danny and I hit it off right away. In addition to seeking various legal reforms, one of the initiatives they discussed with me was their desire to establish a foundation focused on promoting forgiveness. I was happy to give it every support.

I spoke to Danny on the day of Samuel's sentencing. I did so again some months later when Samuel's sentence was reduced on appeal. I think mine was the first call he took. I was in Canberra, and I knew the decision would be handed down that day. When I heard that the sentence had been reduced, I immediately contacted Danny and offered my support and encouragement. Danny was not seeking revenge through the courts, just justice. There is a difference. Like Leila, Danny had also forgiven Samuel. He said he didn't want anger, bitterness, or revenge in his household. In our many conversations, he told me how he didn't want such negativity to prevent him from being the best dad and husband he could be for his family members who were still alive. He said, "Forgiveness and justice go hand in hand, and you can't have one without the other." For him, it was important that our society valued justice, while as believers in Jesus we demonstrated love and forgiveness.

On the first anniversary of the tragedy, the i4give Foundation was launched, with the very first i4give Day on February 1, 2021. It was a great privilege for Danny and Leila to invite me and Jen to speak at the event. Jen does not speak publicly very often, but Leila insisted, and she can be very persuasive. Since then our families have become even closer, with Jen speaking with Leila at all hours, especially when Leila was pregnant with her new baby, Selina, who has now filled the Abdallah house with joy once again. Selina is their seventh child. Danny and Leila are now expecting their eighth child.

Veronique's mother, Bridget, also forgave Samuel, as did her husband, Craig, and Veronique's father, Bob, who has subsequently passed away from cancer. Bridget and Craig have also become our good friends. Bridget shared that she often felt like God had her on "call waiting," but forgiveness helped her to live in the present and not carry anger or hate.

Bridget has established an online prayer platform called heart-FELT for families experiencing loss and trauma. Bridget shared her victim statement with me. It had not been published. Its grace and truth brought me to tears. In her statement, Bridget spoke directly to Samuel and said,

> I have chosen the pathway of showing you mercy. My mercy entails giving you the chance to repent for your horrid actions. My mercy entails that one day accompanied by spiritual directors (priests), that I am granted the opportunity to introduce you to God and his abundant love so that you get the chance to look deep within your heart and soul and call out for help and for God's mercy.
>
> This tragedy is bigger than all of us. Please do not make excuses for your actions and take accountability for killing four innocent children and significantly impacting the other three with their remaining siblings. What does my mercy look like? Mercy is about forgiveness, it is about living with this tragedy embedded in our hearts, soul, and body but without anger attached to me. This frees me up from being chained and dragged into a place where there is only hatred and bitterness. For Jesus in his deepest anguish said while dying on the cross after being scorched and tortured said, "Father, forgive them for they know not what they do."

Wow.

Forgiveness is how these bereft families chose to deal with tragedy. When their faith was put to the test, it produced the forgiveness they needed. From that forgiveness they can now speak of new hope in their lives. They can also speak of a closeness to God they could never previously have imagined.

MY LISTS

Forgiveness is a hard conversation. One night, about ten months after losing the election, I was having a beer with Danny at his place. He put a question to me squarely: "So, Scott," he said, "who do you need to forgive?" It was a confronting question. And if anyone had the right to ask it, it was Danny.

Danny shared with me that night that when Samuel Davidson killed his children, he didn't personally know the man. He said people make mistakes and do stupid, irresponsible, and reckless things. Danny and his family suffered terrible loss because of what Samuel did, but they didn't know him. Amazingly, Danny is now getting to know Samuel in prison; they are talking about Jesus, even with Samuel's family as well. Danny's forgiveness was not just in the moment; it has been ongoing. Danny is now working on restoration and discipling Samuel. I knew I had to take up Danny's challenge and example if I wanted to move forward.

Politics is a tough business. People clash. There is a lot at stake. People lose and people win. Ambitions are thwarted and realized. It tends to be a zero-sum game, as most see it, with no middle ground. In politics I saw a lot of vengeance and bitterness. People nurse grudges yet are usually blind to their own offenses, which mirror what they're complaining about. For some, exacting vengeance becomes their sole purpose. It looked exhausting and, more importantly, pointless. I never understood where they found the time or what they hoped to gain, even when their vengeance was realized. It's been said that vengeance is a dish best served cold, but it leaves the one serving it just as cold.

The road to becoming prime minister and then operating at the highest level of politics is not for the fainthearted. It is unrelenting. Along the way you make mistakes and bitter enemies, you misjudge situations, and you certainly have your regrets. You can't take the field in politics for as long as I have and emerge unscathed, without injury or without having dealt some of your own blows. Thankfully, for me, there were ultimately far more positive experiences, relationships, decisions, and outcomes that I was blessed to be part of. I am thankful for the opportunity to have served God and my country in such a privileged way.

Teddy Roosevelt described what this is like in his speech popularly known as "The Man in the Arena," delivered at the Sorbonne in Paris in 1910.

> It is not the critic who counts; not the man who points out how the strong man stumbles, or where the doer of deeds could have done them better. The credit belongs to the man who is actually in the arena, whose face is marred by dust and sweat and blood; who strives valiantly; who errs, who comes short again and again, because there is no effort without error and shortcoming; but who does actually strive to do the deeds; who knows the great enthusiasms, the great devotions; who spends himself in a worthy cause; who at the best knows in the end the triumph of high achievement, and who at the worst, if he fails, at least fails while daring greatly, so that his place shall never be with those cold and timid souls who neither know victory nor defeat.[14]

Now that I am no longer prime minister, I have had the time to reflect over the many years I spent in the pressure cooker of politics. There are disappointments I have to let go of, where I must pay the price and forgive. There is also repentance I must come to terms with—things I have said, things I could have said better, people I have taken for granted or disappointed, and some policy decisions I regret. Now, I'm not going to turn this into a weeping public confessional; that is not my style. I'm not getting on anyone's couch. Nor is this the point I am making. Those things are between me and God and probably a few others as well, where necessary. My point is not that we should wallow in guilt or public flagellation. My point is about restoration and being able to move forward to the next season.

Working through my repentance and forgiveness lists, I reminded myself of the parable of the unforgiving servant (Matthew 18:21–35) when preparing a message to preach at my home church. To recap the story briefly: Jesus says there is a servant who owes the king a great debt and is about to be sold into slavery, along with his wife and kids. The servant pleads to the king for more time, vowing to do everything he can to repay the debt. The king decides to show mercy and forgive the debt in its entirety. Amazing! The servant is no longer condemned. You'd think this would make him more charitable. Not so. First thing he does is go and shake down another servant who owes him money, refusing to show the same mercy the king showed him. Not surprisingly, this gets the other servants talking and the word reaches the king. The king is not happy. In fact he's furious, and he condemns the unforgiving servant for his unforgiveness.

Jesus said the debt owed by the servant was ten thousand talents. In today's US currency, taking into account average wages, this is almost $400 million.[15] It was an absurd amount—that was Jesus' point. This was an unpayable debt. Forgoing such a large debt would have been a real cost to the king. The king would have been carrying this debt on his balance sheet. Writing off debts of that size costs you (I was a treasurer, remember). The king accepted this. He would have to inject the capital needed to stabilize his balance sheet. He had to pay the price himself to forgive the debt.

The analogy with God, who paid the price through Jesus' death

on the cross to forgive our sins and satisfy the demands of His justice, is obvious to us now. It wouldn't have been so clear to those
to whom Jesus was telling the story. This story was for us, who
now know the reality of being forgiven by God through Jesus. Jesus
is specifically talking to Christians. If we look a little harder at
the actions of the servant who was forgiven, there is another lesson. The servant did not ask for his debt to be canceled. This was
the king's idea. The servant thought all he needed was more time.
Despite the absurdity of the debt he owed, he thought he could pay
it back. We wrongly think we can make some contribution to pay
for our redemption. We cannot. We must just humbly accept our
forgiveness.

It is a mistake to believe that God thinks the way we do. God
wants you to know that you are truly forgiven. If you have repented
and received Jesus' sacrifice for your salvation, your sin can no
longer condemn you. When God says He forgives us, that's it,
once for all (Hebrews 7:27). Our sin is removed as far as the east is
from the west (Psalm 103:12). As Christians we must accept God's
forgiveness and not think it is some sort of layaway (or Afterpay
arrangement, as we call it in Australia). Instead, it's a *Jesuspaid*
arrangement, because Jesus has accepted and paid the debt Himself.
We must accept God's forgiveness in Jesus as absolute, in complete
humility, and with a repentant heart. Once you truly understand
both the impossibility and reality of your forgiveness, the lesson of
the parable is that you can do nothing other than be compelled to
forgive others. God wants you to forgive as He forgave you.

This is such a challenging parable from Jesus because there are
few among us, if any, who could claim to be anything other than the
unforgiving servant in this story. Unless we have truly forgiven all
those who have ever injured us and are loving our enemies and praying for them to prosper and succeed, then we are the unforgiving

servant. It is true that I have experienced deep hurt and unfairness, especially in my political life. As a Christian, however, there is no justification in not forgiving these injuries. Regardless of what others may have done to me, God has already forgiven me so much more that I cannot even comprehend the scale of the debt I owe to God for my salvation. How can I therefore dwell on those who have sinned against me and refuse to forgive them? I'm working on it.

SUFFICIENT GRACE

In 2023, Danny, Leila, and the i4give team organized a family festival at a local park in Parramatta in western Sydney. It was a beautiful day. There were carnival rides, stalls, a stage, musical performers, face painters, the works. Rather than dwelling on the hurt of losing family, they chose to turn this into a day of joy to celebrate family that ended with an open-air family movie screening.

Four paths led to the center of the park where the stage was set. As you walked down each of those paths toward the stage, large floral arches stretched over each pathway. The arches were swollen with flowers. At the top of each arch was the name of one of their kids: Antony, Angelina, Sienna, and Veronique. It really was something. At the rear of the stage was a massive floral backdrop in the shape of a heart made of roses with "i4give" written in the middle.

Even though the new prime minister and state premier had been appropriately invited to speak at the event, Leila insisted I also speak. This time I was not there as a politician but as a friend who was on the journey with them. Just like in previous years, we had gone along as a family with Abbey and Lily. This year we were all dressed in our i4give team T-shirts. That day I spoke even more from the heart, no longer having to be cautious about blurring the lines between faith and politics. I said that people would often ask me and Jen about Danny and Leila and how they could forgive the man who had killed their children. I said there was no explanation other than the impact of Jesus on their lives. Their forgiveness was not a self-evident instinctive human response. In fact, it was quite the opposite. The human response would have been to strike out, to punish and seek vengeance. This would have destroyed them. Instead, the families forgave out of the instinctive obedience of their faith, which they had received from their relationship with Jesus. Their forgiveness set them free.

I read from Paul's second letter to the Corinthians, where Paul spoke of how Jesus told him, "My grace is sufficient for you, for [God's] power is perfected in weakness" (12:9). I said I could not have imagined a weaker moment than your children being taken from you in the way Antony, Angelique, Sienna, and Veronique were taken from their families. Yet in their moment of weakness, God's grace was sufficient and it remained. God's power enabled them to endure, to forgive and move forward. Each day is still a challenge, but these families are living in the power God made perfect in their own weakness. One day, the families will be reunited with their children. When they all get together, it will be amazing. Jen and I are also looking forward to meeting them all one day.

Forgiveness is the fruit of our faith and relationship with Jesus Christ.

Forgiveness is the fruit of our faith and relationship with Jesus Christ. Forgiveness may be too much for us, but it's not too much for God. Few things will hold you back and block the flow of God's presence and blessing in our lives more than our reluctance to forgive. But nothing screams the love of God louder than forgiveness.

EPILOGUE

But as for me, I will be on the watch for the LORD;
I will wait for the God of my salvation.
My God will hear me.
MICAH 7:7

On Sunday morning I walked up to the main marquee that hosted all our big camp gatherings. It was a giant circus tent. More than eight hundred boys had come from all over Australia and overseas for the 7th Pan Australian Boys' Brigade Camp. It was being held at Nunawading, an outer suburb of Melbourne. It had been a fun week: obstacle courses, rugby, cricket, hiking—lots of boy stuff. I was twelve years old.

Throughout the week, a chaplain in our section of the camp had been leading Bible studies. I had been quietly paying attention. I filed inside the big tent for the Sunday church service with all the other boys and sat near one of the big pylons holding up the marquee. I was sitting about three-quarters of the way toward the back of the tent. There were the usual songs. The camp chaplain gave a sermon. I don't remember what he said or if I even found it persuasive. What happened next was not the result of some logical or intellectual process. It was something else entirely. At the end of the service, the chaplain asked if anyone wanted to give their life to Jesus as their Lord and Savior. He said to stand in your place and join him in a prayer. The next thing I knew, I was standing, as if someone had pulled me to my feet, but I didn't resist. I gave my life to the Lord there and then. It was Sunday, January 11, 1981.

As I walked out of the marquee, I knew something unlike anything I had ever experienced had just happened. I looked up. The sky was a brilliant blue. There was a gentle breeze. It was like I was connected to heaven itself. There was a brightness I could not explain. Everything slowed down. My senses were overloaded. I could feel heaven rejoicing. I knew I would never be the same.

I spent the rest of the day with our section chaplain, who explained a few more things to me about what had just happened. I couldn't get enough of what he was telling me. My journey with Jesus had begun.

In the Old Testament, it was common to place stones to mark significant moments and places where God had led and provided for the people of Israel. When stones were laid down, they were often given a name. For example, in Genesis 28:10–16 we read about Jacob's dream where he saw a ladder extending into heaven with angels going up and down. God was standing at the top and said to him, "I am with you and will keep you wherever you go, and will bring you back to this land; for I will not leave you until I have done what I have promised you." Unsurprisingly, Jacob woke up the following day and said, "The LORD is certainly in this place." He said the place was awesome and described it as the gate of heaven. He took the stone he had used for a pillow, poured oil on it, and called the place Bethel, which means "house of God."

My friend Pastor Michael Murphy reminded me of another

such stone, the Ebenezer stone (1 Samuel 7:12–13). Samuel had told the Israelites that if they were serious about returning to God, they had to get rid of all the idols they had been worshiping. The Message translation says they had to "clean house," which they did. Samuel then called them together at Mizpah, where he said he would pray for them. The Philistines heard that the Israelites were all together in one place and saw this as an opportunity to attack. The Israelites learned that the Philistines were on their way. Scripture says they became frightened and pleaded with Samuel to pray all the more, which he did. When the Philistines came within range of their attack, God showed up. A huge thunderclap exploded among the Philistines, causing panic and mass confusion, scattering their forces, enabling the Israelites to pursue them and strike them down and win a great victory. The Bible then says that Samuel took a single rock and set it upright and named it Ebenezer, which means "Rock of Help," saying, "So far the LORD has helped us" (v. 13).

It is good to lay down stones of remembrance along our journey with God to remind us just how far God has brought us. The stones show us how God's plans have, in fact, been for our good. They also remind us of some of the extremes God has pushed us to in order to show His provision, love, strength, grace, and power. This far God has helped us, we can say, as Samuel did. These stones are also a testimony to others about the goodness of God in our lives. It would have been fitting for me to have laid a stone on that day I gave my life to Jesus at Nunawading. In many ways, each chapter of this book has represented such a stone, laid down to mark the moments of God's presence in my own journey as I have walked with Jesus for more than forty years now.

There is no checkbox formula for life. If only life were that easy. It's not. We are all complex. Our situations and experiences are unique. When you listen carefully and lean in to God, you will hear

His whisper. That is what Jesus promised the Holy Spirit would do (John 14:16–17; 26). I hope and pray that in these pages there has been at least one message or lesson that may have resonated with you.

For me, I keep coming back to the thought that if you can't trust God with everything, you can't trust God with anything. Our faith is not a pastime. It is not an opinion. Our faith is not a vending machine. It is not our politics. Our faith is not a philosophy, a way of looking at the world, or even how we try to explain it. It is much more personal than this. Our faith is life itself, and it is through the activation of our faith in the gospel of Jesus Christ that we have gained access to the everlasting grace (unmerited favor) of God. This has brought us into an eternal and loving personal relationship with God that was previously impossible. This was made possible by the sacrifice of Jesus Christ on the cross and His resurrection from the dead. In this relationship, we are forgiven; our identity is secured; our purpose is established; our fears and anxieties are overwhelmed by His power and peace; His inexhaustible love bears our sorrow and sustains us. That is the experience I can testify to.

On so many occasions, I have come back to God's promise in Jeremiah 29:11: "'For I know the plans that I have for you,' declares the LORD, 'plans for prosperity and not for disaster, to give you a future and a hope.'" At the end of the day, we have to decide whether we believe this is true or not. If we believe it, we can claim the future and hope that God has promised us. And if we believe, then we are called to act on that faith, to believe in miracles, to love, to forgive, to repent, to surrender, to obey, to serve, to worship, and to follow.

The life of such faith is not easy, but take heart, because God understands that we struggle with this journey. Jesus demonstrated this to us in the gracious way that He dealt with His disciples. He loved them. He chose them. He knew their flaws and weaknesses, but He also knew their heart for Him and their faith. He knew they would fail. He even assured them they would, telling Peter he would deny Him three times. He was patient with them. He built them up, restored them when they were down, and admonished and consoled them when He needed to. He understood their humanity, just like He understands ours.

In John 21 we read that after Jesus' resurrection, He went to Galilee where Peter and John had returned and had gone fishing, just like they used to when Jesus first found Peter. It had been a terrible night. They had caught nothing. Jesus was watching them from the beach. They hadn't yet recognized Him. Jesus suggested they go back and cast their nets on the other side and they would catch some fish. Sound familiar? They did, just as they had done around three years before, when Peter's journey with Jesus began. The boat was almost swamped by the haul of fish they brought up. John, once again referring to himself as the one Jesus loved, said he told Peter it was Jesus on the shore. Peter could not contain himself. Peter threw himself into the water and thrashed his way back to the shore to see Jesus.

As he made his way to the shore, I can imagine Peter playing back in his mind the incredible events of the past three years—the blessings, the trials, the miracles, his denial. They sat down and had a seafood BBQ by the beach. Jesus had not come to rebuke Peter for denying Him. Jesus didn't ask Peter, "Why did you sin against Me?" or "Why did you let Me down?" or "Why did you forget Me?" Jesus only had one question, but He asked it three times—perhaps once for each denial: "Do you love Me?" (verses 16–17). On each occasion Peter answered yes. Jesus then commissioned Peter and concluded by saying to him, "Follow Me" (verse 19). If we love Jesus, then we must follow Him.

Following Jesus does not come without a cost. In that same beachside conversation, Jesus alluded to how Peter would one day be put to death for his faith. Some years later, Peter wrote to the Christians scattered throughout various parts of Asia, referring to them as aliens or strangers (1 Peter 1:1). In my public life, I have often felt like an alien in the place where I believed God had called me to serve. I think this alien experience is how many Christians feel about living in our Western society today.

Our world is changing. Christianity has been the dominant culture of Western society for over fifteen hundred years. However, our culture now increasingly acts as if it has outgrown God. As a society, we have become wise in our own eyes. We pretend to have knowledge and insight that, somehow, we think has eluded the eternal God. Arrogance and pride have taken the place of humility and reverence before God. The eternal and immutable standards of God are now being substituted for what we believe is right in our own eyes (Judges 21:25). The truth is now as we each seek to define it. How convenient for us.

In such a world Christians will increasingly face trials, discrimination, mocking, and persecution, as Jesus said we would (John 16:33). In such a world we are right to feel like aliens if we are truly holding to our faith. How much more important, then, that we hold to our faith in these times?

About a year after the election loss, Danny gave me a painting of Daniel praying in the lions' den. He told me that this is what he thought it must have felt like when I was prime minister. He was right. As Christians in a society that is increasingly hostile to our faith, the lesson of Daniel is a good one for us to follow. Rather than react as the world reacts, Daniel trusted in God's eternal plan. He stood and served where God had placed him, as an alien. The good news is that God's got this. Daniel understood this.

God's purposes are greater than those we currently see impacting our society.

The message and instruction from our God have not changed. We are to wait on the Lord and live out our faith in His love. God has already won the victory. As it says in Scripture, we are to love God with all our heart, our soul, and our minds, and we are to love one another (Matthew 22:37–40). That is our calling.

Whatever our times or our experiences, we will see the goodness of God's plans in our lives if we choose to seek Him, if we choose to trust Him, and if we choose to love and follow Him. When we do this, we can look back on the many stones that have been laid down across our lives, signifying His great blessing and faithfulness, and rejoice. These stones do not just remind us to give thanks. These stones lead us onward, confirming God's plans for our good and that the best is always yet to come. *Amen.*

ACKNOWLEDGMENTS

First, I want to thank you for taking the time to read or listen to this book. I pray it will help you along your path. I hope we can continue our conversation again soon.

With any first book, you need a lot of help. There is a lot to learn, especially about the writing process and the publishing business. I am very grateful to all the team at HarperCollins Christian Publishing for their patience, enthusiasm, belief, and support for this project, especially Mark Schoenwald and Damon Reiss. This was never going to be a usual book for a politician, and Mark and Damon understood this right from the start.

I first met my amazing editor, Lisa-Jo Baker, in Washington, DC, in December 2022. Lisa-Jo had read a rough draft of some early chapters. She got it immediately. Lisa-Jo and I were meant to do this book together. Hopefully we'll do more. Thanks also to Rod Storer for bringing his insight, talents, and experience to this project and to the rest of the editing team. A special thanks also to my literary agent, David Vigliano, for helping me with my "known unknowns" in the publishing business. He had it covered, which meant I could just focus on the work.

There were also a lot of volunteer contributors to the project. Thanks to Pastors Valerie and Michael Murphy, Dr. Anne Knock, Lucy Wicks, Andrew Carswell, and Pastor Kristy Mills for laboring through my early drafts and giving me great feedback. A very special thank-you to my "big sister" cousin, Dr. Susan Bradley Smith. Susie is a gifted poet, academic, and published author. She gave me the confidence and expert advice I needed to take this on.

Of course, none of what I have spoken of in this work would have been possible without the many people God has put in my life to share this journey.

As a politician, you are the tip of the spear. I have been blessed throughout my political career with incredibly loyal, capable, and committed staff. From my local office team and supporters in the Shire, especially Julie Adams, to the incredible professionals who headed up and worked in my prime ministerial and ministerial offices, in particular Dr. John Kunkel and my long-standing executive assistant, Latisha Wenlock. There are too many of you to mention all by name, but I hope you all feel the full partnership of our service together and what we were able to contribute. Thanks also to my many party, parliamentary, and ministerial colleagues with whom I served over the years, who provided great friendship and encouragement, in particular Michael McCormack, Josh Frydenberg, Greg Hunt, Ben Morton, Steve Irons, Stuart Robert, Alex Hawke, Lucy Wicks, Bill Heffernan, Louise Markus, and Shane Stone.

I am also grateful for the great Christian friendship of US Vice President Mike Pence, US Secretary of State Mike Pompeo, and Prime Minister James Marape from Papua New Guinea.

When I entered politics, a former member of Parliament gave some good advice about making sure you did not neglect the friendships you had before you came into office. I took this advice seriously. I am even more pleased that my friends did the same. Thank you to our wonderful friends Karen and Adrian Harrington, David Gazard, Arthur and Ingrid Ilias, Bill and Anne Knock, Peter Verwer, Scott Briggs, and Lynelle Stewart. To my pastors Brad Bonhomme, Mike Murphy, Joel A'bell, and Jock Cameron, as well as my brothers in Christ Andrew Scipione, John Anderson, and Lloyd Thomas, thank you for your prayers, counsel, and encouragement. Thanks also to Pastor Margaret Court, Bishop Antoine Tarabay, and all of our Maronite brothers and sisters, especially Danny and Leila Abdallah, Bridget Sakr, and Craig McKenzie.

As you will have noted from this book, subject only to God, my family is the center of my life. At the very center of our family is Jen, to whom I have singularly dedicated this work. I cannot imagine life without her. Jen is the other half of our joined soul, who, by the grace of God, brought Abbey and Lily, our miracle girls, into our lives, whom we celebrate and love. I thank Abbey and Lily for their own sacrifices necessitated by having a father in public life. Thank you also to Jen's mum, Beth; her late father, Roy; and her siblings Garry and Cecily and all their families. Finally, I thank my mum, Marion; my late dad, John; and my older brother, Alan. I would never have known God and Jesus Christ if it were not for them. I could think of no greater gift.

ABOUT THE AUTHOR

Scott Morrison served as Australia's 30th Prime Minister (2018–2022), and in other senior Cabinet posts for almost nine years. Prime Minister Scott founded the historic AUKUS defense agreement between Australia, the United Kingdom, and the United States and delivered one of the most effective responses to the global COVID-19 pandemic in the developed world. Post-politics, Scott now serves on a series of global corporate and think tank advisory boards, advising on geopolitics, infrastructure, defense, and security issues. Scott lives with his wife, Jenny, and two teenage daughters in Sydney, Australia, where they are part of Horizon Church, a local evangelical Christian community.

NOTES

PREFACE

1. Erik Larson, *The Splendid and the Vile: A Saga of Churchill, Family, and Defiance During the Blitz* (London: William Collins, 2020), 96.
2. Fanny Crosby and Phoebe Knapp, "Blessed Assurance," 1873, Hymnary.org, https://hymnary.org/text/blessed_assurance_jesus _is_mine.

CHAPTER 2

1. "ScoMo's Miracle," *Brisbane Sunday Mail*, May 19, 2019, 1.

CHAPTER 3

1. Jonathan Sacks, *Morality: Restoring the Common Good in Divided Times* (London: Hodder and Stoughton, 2020), 39; Jonathan Sacks, *The Great Partnership: Science, Religion, and the Search for Meaning* (New York: Schocken Books, 2011), 127.
2. Jonathan Sacks, "The Environment of Faith—BBC Reith Lectures 1990: The Persistence of Faith—Lecture 1," The Rabbi Sacks Legacy Trust, November 14, 1990, https://soundcloud.com/office-of -rabbi-sacks/rla-jonathan-sacks-the-5.
3. Sacks, *Great Partnership*, 36, 291–95.

4. Rick Warren, *The Purpose Driven Life: What on Earth Am I Here For?* (Grand Rapids, MI: Zondervan, 2002).

5. Jonathan Sacks, *Lessons in Leadership: A Weekly Reading of the Jewish Bible* (Jerusalem: Maggid Books, 2015), 297.

CHAPTER 4

1. "William Roberts (1757–1820)," People Australia, National Centre of Biography, Australian National University, accessed April 18, 2023, https://peopleaustralia.anu.edu.au/biography/roberts-william -27348/text34807.

2. Phil Hands, "William Roberts," Convict Records, March 27, 2023, https://convictrecords.com.au/convicts/roberts/william/134639.

3. Elizabeth Kotlowski, *Stories of Australia's Christian Heritage: Explorers, Colonial Times, Pioneers, Statesmen* (Sydney: Strand, 2006), 25.

4. Kotlowski, *Stories of Australia's Christian Heritage*, 25.

5. "Kezia Roberts (1771–1854)," People Australia, National Centre of Biography, Australian National University, accessed April 18, 2023, https://peopleaustralia.anu.edu.au/biography/roberts-kezia-27349 /text34808.

6. Watkin Tench, *1788,* ed. Tim Flannery, Text Classics (Melbourne: Text Publishing Company, 2012), 132.

7. Noel Goss, "Our Australia: The Second Fleet," *The Argus* (Melbourne), January 27, 1940, 8.

8. See the Australian Institute of Aboriginal and Torres Strait Islander Studies, www.aiatsis.gov.au.

9. "William Roberts," Fellowship of First Fleeters, accessed April 18, 2023, http://www.fellowshipfirstfleeters.org.au/william_roberts.htm.

10. Commonwealth of Australia Const., Compilation No. 6 (1977), https://www.legislation.gov.au/Details/C2013Q00005.

11. Census of the Commonwealth of Australia (1961), Australian Bureau of Statistics, https://www.abs.gov.au/ausstats/abs@.nsf/mf /2107.0.

12. "2001 Census Data," Australian Bureau of Statistics, accessed September 18, 2023, https://www.abs.gov.au/websitedbs/census home.nsf/home/historicaldata2001?opendocument.

13. "2001 Census Data."

14. "2021 Census Shows Changes in Australia's Religious Diversity," Australian Bureau of Statistics, June 28, 2022, https://www.abs .gov.au/media-centre/media-releases/2021-census-shows-changes -australias-religious-diversity.

15. Religion, England and Wales: Census 2021, UK Office for National Statistics, https://www.ons.gov.uk/peoplepopulationandcommunity /culturalidentity/religion/bulletins/religionenglandandwales/census 2021; D. Clark, "Religious Identification in Scotland in 2018," Statista, July 20, 2023, https://www.statista.com/statistics/367848 /scotland-religious-beliefs-population/; "Losing Our Religion," StatsNZ, October 3, 2019, https://www.stats.govt.nz/news/losing -our-religion.

16. "Religion in Canada," Statistics Canada, October 28, 2021, https:// www150.statcan.gc.ca/n1/pub/11–627-m/11–627-m2021079-eng .htm.

17. PRRI Staff, "2021 PRRI Census of American Religion, Updates and Trends: White Christian Decline Slows, Unaffiliated Growth Levels Off," Public Religion Research Institute, April 27, 2022, https:// www.prri.org/spotlight/prri-2021-american-values-atlas-religious -affiliation-updates-and-trends-white-christian-decline-slows -unaffiliated-growth-levels-off/.

18. Rod Dreher, *The Benedict Option: A Strategy for Christians in a Post-Christian Nation* (New York: Penguin Random House, 2017), 36.

19. Dreher, *Benedict Option*, 36.

20. Dreher, *Benedict Option*, 37.

21. Jonathan Sacks, *The Great Partnership: Science, Religion, and the Search for Meaning* (New York: Schocken Books, 2011), 102, 109.

22. Aleksandr Solzhenitsyn, *The Gulag Archipelago 1918–1956: An*

Experiment in Literary Investigation, vol. 2 (New York: Harper and Row, 1975), 615.

23. Jordan B. Peterson, *12 Rules for Life: An Antidote to Chaos* (New York: Penguin, 2019), 144.

24. Peterson, *12 Rules for Life,* 158.

25. Peterson, *12 Rules for Life,* 109.

26. Peterson, *12 Rules for Life,* 109.

27. Sacks, *Great Partnership,* 259.

28. Greg Lukianoff and Jonathan Haidt, *The Coddling of the American Mind: How Good Intentions and Bad Ideas Are Setting Up a Generation for Failure* (New York: Penguin Press, 2018).

29. Lukianoff and Haidt, *Coddling of the American Mind,* 6.

30. C. S. Lewis, *Mere Christianity* (London: William Collins, 2012), 56.

31. Richard Stearns, *The Hole in Our Gospel: What Does God Expect of Us? The Answer That Changed My Life and Might Just Change the World* (Nashville, TN: W Publishing, 2009), xxi.

32. Dreher, *Benedict Option,* 99.

33. "Final Report," Royal Commission into Institutional Responses to Child Sexual Abuse, accessed September 18, 2023, https://www.child abuseroyalcommission.gov.au/final-report.

34. "National Apology," National Office for Child Safety, Australian Government, accessed April 20, 2023, https://www.childsafety.gov .au/royal-commission/national-apology.

35. Nicci Gemmel, "Hard-Line Religion? Young People Look On in Bewilderment and Revulsion," *The Australian,* November 5, 2022.

CHAPTER 5

1. *Chariots of Fire,* directed by Hugh Hudson (Los Angeles: 20th Century Fox, 1981).

2. *Compass,* "Cronulla to Kokoda," presented by Geraldine Doogue, broadcast July 8, 2007, by Australian Broadcasting Corporation, https://www.abc.net.au/religion/watch/compass/compass-cronulla -to-kokoda/10143374.

CHAPTER 6

1. *Bridge of Spies*, directed by Steven Spielberg (Universal City, CA: DreamWorks Pictures, 2015).

2. Damien Cave, "How Australia Saved Thousands of Lives While COVID Killed a Million Americans," *New York Times*, May 15, 2022, https://www.nytimes.com/2022/05/15/world/australia/covid-deaths.html.

3. Our World in Data, Global Change Data Lab, accessed July 13, 2022, https://ourworldindata.org.

4. Parl. Deb. H. R. (August 25, 2020), 5431, https://www.aph.gov.au/Parliamentary_Business/Hansard/Hansard_Display?bid=chamber/hansardr/f2b4d1a9–30b7–4ee1-ab7b-0ca667d8dfb6/&sid=0080. (Answer based on advice provided by the Australian Government Department of Health.)

5. Megan Sauer, "Bill Gates: 'If Every Country Does What Australia Did,' the World Could Prevent the Next Pandemic," CNBC, February 24, 2022, https://www.cnbc.com/2022/02/24/bill-gates-australia-covid-blueprint-could-help-prevent-next-pandemic.html.

6. Sauer, "Bill Gates."

7. "2021 GHS Index Country Profile for Australia," Global Health Security Index, accessed April 20, 2023, https://www.ghsindex.org/country/australia/.

8. "National Accounts," Australian Bureau of Statistics, https://www.abs.gov.au/statistics/economy/national-accounts. See June Quarter 2022 and December Quarter 2019.

9. See "OECD National Accounts Statistics," OECD iLibrary, https://www.oecd-ilibrary.org/economics/data/oecd-national-accounts-statistics/quarterly-national-accounts_data-00017-en.

10. "OECD National Accounts Statistics."

11. "Labour Force, Australia," Australian Bureau of Statistics, May 2022, https://www.abs.gov.au/statistics/labour/employment-and-unemployment/labour-force-australia/may-2022.

12. S&P Global Ratings, Fitch Ratings, Moody's.

13. "Suicide and Self Harm Monitoring," Australian Institute of Health and Welfare, accessed September 18, 2023, https://www.aihw.gov .au/suicide-self-harm-monitoring/data/data-downloads. See "Data Tables: 2021 National Mortality Database—Suicide (ICD-10 X60–X84, Y87.0)."

14. "Long-Term Health Conditions," Australian Bureau of Statistics, August 20, 2022, https://www.abs.gov.au/articles/long-term-health -conditions.

15. "National Study of Mental Health and Wellbeing," Australian Bureau of Statistics, July 22, 2022, https://www.abs.gov.au /statistics/health/mental-health/national-study-mental-health-and -wellbeing/latest-release.

16. "National Study of Mental Health and Wellbeing."

17. *Key Substance Use and Mental Health Indicators in the United States: Results from the 2020 National Survey on Drug Use and Health*, (Rockville, MD: Center for Behavioral Health Statistics and Quality, Substance Abuse and Mental Health Services Administration, 2021), https://www.samhsa.gov/data/sites/default /files/reports/rpt35325/NSDUHFFRPDFWHTMLFiles2020/2020 NSDUHFFR1PDFW102121.pdf.

18. *Protecting Your Mental Health: The U.S. Surgeon General's Advisory*, (Washington, DC: Office of the Surgeon General, US Department of Health and Human Services, 2021), https://www .hhs.gov/sites/default/files/surgeon-general-youth-mental-health -advisory.pdf.

19. *Protecting Your Mental Health.*

20. *Key Substance Use and Mental Health Indicators.*

21. *Australian Story*, season 22, episode 30, "Beyond OK," broadcast September 4, 2017, on Australian Broadcasting Corporation, broadcast September 4, 2017, https://www.abc.net.au/news/2017–09 –04/beyond-ok:-the-story-of-the-man-behind-r-u-ok-day/8866798.

22. Louise Brådvik, "Suicide Risk and Mental Disorders," *International*

Journal of Environmental Research and Public Health 15, no. 9 (2018), https://doi.org/10.3390/ijerph15092028.

CHAPTER 7

1. "Address: Launch of the 2020 Defence Strategic Update," PM Transcripts, Department of the Prime Minister and Cabinet, July 1, 2020, https://pmtranscripts.pmc.gov.au/release/transcript-42881.

2. Xi Jinping, "Address to the Parliament of Australia" (speech), November 17, 2014, Commonwealth Parliament of Australia, House of Representatives.

3. Graham Allison, "What Xi Jinping Wants," *The Atlantic*, May 31, 2017, https://www.theatlantic.com/international/archive/2017/05/what-china-wants/528561/.

4. *Military and Security Developments Involving the People's Republic of China 2022*, (Washington, DC: US Department of Defense, 2022) https://media.defense.gov/2022/Nov/29/2003122279/-1/-1/1/2022-Military-And-Security-Developments-Involving-The-Peoples-Republic-Of-China.pdf.

5. *Military and Security Developments*, 45.

6. *Military and Security Developments*, 50–53.

7. *Military and Security Developments*, 51, 55.

8. *Military and Security Developments*, 53.

9. *Military and Security Developments*, 59.

10. *Military and Security Developments*, 94.

11. *Military and Security Developments*, 64–66, 82–83.

12. Timothy Keller, "No One Seeks God—Romans 3:9–20," sermon, March 1, 2009, Redeemer Presbyterian Church (New York), https://www.monergism.com/no-one-seeks-god-romans-39-20.

CHAPTER 8

1. Anne Henderson, *Joseph Lyons: The People's Prime Minister* (Sydney: NewSouth Publishing, 2011).

CHAPTER 9

1. *The Digital Encyclopedia of George Washington*, Mount Vernon Ladies' Association, s.v. "Conway Cabal," by James Scythes, accessed April 20, 2023, https://www.mountvernon.org/library /digitalhistory/digital-encyclopedia/article/conway-cabal/.

2. "Exhibit Overview," Valley Forge National Historical Park, ParkNet, accessed September 18, 2023, https://www.nps.gov/museum/exhibits /revwar/vafo/vafooverview.html.

3. George Washington, "Letter to Brigadier General Casimir Pulaski, December 31, 1777," The Papers of George Washington Digital Edition, University of Virginia.

4. Rick Herrera and Ron Granieri, "Countering the Myths of Valley Forge," War Room, March 22, 2023, https://warroom.armywar college.edu/podcasts/valley-forge/.

5. Ricardo A. Herrera, "'Our Army Will Hut This Winter at Valley Forge': George Washington, Decision Making, and the Councils of War," *Army History* 117 (Fall 2020): 6–27, https://www.jstor.org /stable/26939904.

6. Ron Chernow, *Washington: A Life* (New York: Penguin, 2010), 323–24.

7. Chernow, *Washington*.

8. Ricardo A. Herrera, "Foraging and Combat Operations at Valley Forge February–March 1778: February–March 1778," *Army History* 79 (Spring 2011): 6–29, https://www.jstor.org/stable /26296823.

9. "Baron von Steuben," American Battlefield Trust, accessed September 18, 2023, https://www.battlefields.org/learn/biographies /baron-von-steuben.

10. *The Digital Encyclopedia of George Washington*, Mount Vernon Ladies' Association, s.v. "Marquis de Lafayette," by Mary Stockwell, accessed April 20, 2023, https://www.mountvernon.org/library /digitalhistory/digital-encyclopedia/article/marquis-de-lafayette/.

11. "Winter at Valley Forge," American Battlefield Trust, September 21, 2017, https://www.battlefields.org/learn/articles/winter-valley-forge.
12. Chernow, *Washington*, 324.
13. Ron Chernow, *Alexander Hamilton* (New York: Penguin, 2004), 107.
14. Chernow, *Washington*, 324.
15. Oxford Reference, "Harold Wilson 1916–95," accessed September 18, 2023, https://www.oxfordreference.com/display/10.1093/acref/9780191843730.001.0001/q-oro-ed5–00011621?rskey=r76rRU&result=1.
16. "Endometriosis," Johns Hopkins Medicine, accessed April 25, 2023, https://www.hopkinsmedicine.org/health/conditions-and-diseases/endometriosis.
17. "Endometriosis."
18. Claire Armstrong, "Jenny Morrison Welcomes Coalition's $58m for Endometriosis Treatment," *Daily Telegraph*, March 24, 2022, https://www.dailytelegraph.com.au/news/nsw/jenny-morrison-welcomes-coalitions-58m-for-endometriosis-treatment/news-story/230952b3b6a20c642b453baebd9b495f.
19. "Endometriosis."

CHAPTER 10

1. "How Keith Got His Start," Tamworth Country Music Festival, January 5, 2022, https://www.tcmf.com.au/how-keith-got-his-start.
2. "How Keith Got His Start."
3. "Colin (Col) Hardy (1940–?)," Indigenous Australia, National Centre of Biography, Australian National University, accessed September 18, 2023, https://ia.anu.edu.au/biography/hardy-colin-col-31740.
4. "Brewarrina Aboriginal Fish Traps (Baiame's Ngunnhu), Doyle St, Brewarrina, NSW, Australia," Department of Climate Change, Energy, the Environment and Water, Australian Government,

accessed September 18, 2023, http://www.environment.gov.au/cgi
-bin/ahdb/search.pl?mode=place_detail;place_id=105778.

5. G. M. Smith, "Pioneers of the West: The Massacre at Hospital
Creek," *Sydney Mail*, September 12, 1923, https://trove.nla.gov.au
/newspaper/article/158404490.

6. "Ubuntu" is "the idea that people are not only individuals but live
in a community and must share things and care for each other."
Oxford Learner's Dictionaries, s.v. "ubuntu," https://www.oxford
learnersdictionaries.com/us/definition/english/ubuntu.

7. John Allen, *Rabble-Rouser for Peace: The Authorized Biography of
Desmond Tutu* (London: Ebury: Rider, 2006), 344.

8. *New World Encyclopedia*, "Ubuntu (philosophy)," accessed
October 29, 2023, https://www.newworldencyclopedia.org/p/index
.php?title=Ubuntu_(philosophy)&oldid=1111253.

9. Allen, *Rabble-Rouser for Peace*, 345.

10. Timothy Keller, *Forgive: Why Should I and How Can I?* (London:
Hodder and Stoughton, 2022), 89.

11. Keller, *Forgive*, 78.

12. Keller, *Forgive*, 90.

13. Jonathan Hair, "Oatlands Drunk Driver Samuel Davidson Jailed
for 28 Years over Crash That Killed Four Children," ABC News,
April 8, 2021, https://www.abc.net.au/news/2021–04–09/drunk
-driver-samuel-davidson-jailed-for-oatlands-crash/100057958.

14. Theodore Roosevelt, "The Man in the Arena" (speech), April 23,
1910, via Theodore Roosevelt Center at Dickinson State University,
transcript, https://www.theodorerooseveltcenter.org/Learn-About
-TR/TR-Encyclopedia/Culture-and-Society/Man-in-the-Arena.aspx.

15. Keller, *Forgive*, 5.